John Wesley
and Marriage

John Wesley and Marriage

Bufford W. Coe

Lehigh
University
Press

Bethlehem
Lehigh University Press
London: Associated University Presses

Associated University Presses
440 Forsgate Drive
Cranbury, NJ 08512

Associated University Presses
25 Sicilian Avenue
London WC1A 2QH, England

Associated University Presses
P.O. Box 338, Port Credit
Mississauga, Ontario
Canada L5G 4L8

The paper used in this publication meets the requirements
of the American National Standard for Permanence of Paper
for Printed Library Materials Z39.48-1984.

Library of Congress Cataloging-in-Publication Data

Coe, Bufford W., 1951–
    John Wesley and marriage / Bufford W. Coe.
        p.   cm.
    Includes bibliographical references and index.
    ISBN 0-934223-39-4 (alk. paper)
    1. Marriage—Religious aspects—Methodist Church—History of doctrines—18th century.   2. Marriage—Religious aspects—Church of England—History of doctrines—18th century.   3. Wesley, John, 1703–1791–Contributions in doctrine of marriage.   4. Wesley, John, 1703–1791.   Sunday service of the Methodists in North America. 5. Church of England—Doctrines—History—18th century. 6. Methodist Church—Doctrines   History—18th century.   7. Anglican Communion—England—Doctrines—History—18th century.   8. Methodist Church—Liturgy—History—18th century.   9. Church of England—Liturgy—History—18th century.   10. Anglican Communion—England—Liturgy—History—18th century.   I. Title.
BX8349.M35C64   1996
264'.07085—dc20   95-35746
                                                                              CIP

PRINTED IN THE UNITED STATES OF AMERICA

To Genie,
who made it possible

Contents

Introduction

In 1784 John Wesley published *The Sunday Service of the Methodists in North America with Other Occasional Services*. This was Wesley's revision of the Anglican Book of Common Prayer for the use of American Methodists in the new political and ecclesiastical situation created by the recent American War of Independence. Later editions of the *Sunday Service* were published for use in Great Britain itself and "in His Majesty's Dominions" overseas.[1] Wesley made a number of deletions and changes in the prayer book while producing the *Sunday Service*; in fact, the *Sunday Service* is only slightly over half as long as the 1662 edition of the Book of Common Prayer on which it was based.[2] But despite having excised so much material from the prayer book, Wesley himself maintained that his revision was a conservative one and that he had been reluctant to make unnecessary changes. In a letter dated 20 June 1789 Wesley wrote, "I took particular care throughout, to alter nothing merely for altering's [sic] sake. In religion, I am for as few innovations as possible. I love the old wine best."[3]

In light of this statement, the changes that Wesley made in the prayer book take on increased significance as indications of his liturgical theology and preferences. By comparing the *Sunday Service* with the 1662 Book of Common Prayer, scholars have gained valuable insight into Wesley's liturgical thought. Nolan Harmon, one of the pioneers of such study, explains its significance.

> . . . the strokes of Wesley's pen in "killing" material he did not want the printer to reproduce, were *positive* strokes, not simply a casual elision of material for the sake of abridgement. We often find in Wesley's omissions a powerful "argument from silence," paradoxical as that sounds, but the silence does not speak unless one knows exactly what Wesley's omissions were.[4]

Most studies of the *Sunday Service* have focused on Wesley's orders for morning prayer, Eucharist, baptism, and ordination. Far less attention has been paid to the "occasional services," such as matrimony and the burial of the dead.

It is the order for matrimony which is the subject of this study. Why did Wesley make the changes that he did in the marriage service from the Book of Common Prayer? Why did he delete the words he deleted and retain the words he retained? What is the relationship between Wesley's liturgical design for matrimony and his thoughts on marriage expressed in his other writings? And finally, what, if anything, can Wesley teach the contemporary church about ministering to persons at this crucial point in their lives?

The components of Wesley's marriage liturgy from the *Sunday Service* are discussed under thematic headings rather than in order of their appearance in the service. Each of these elements of the service has been studied in light of Wesley's other writings in an effort to determine why Wesley revised the Anglican wedding service in the way that he did. Background information on eighteenth-century social history, economics, and politics is introduced as needed in order to understand the context in which Wesley worked.

The first chapter examines the legal context of marriage. When presiding at a wedding, the minister serves a dual role: he or she is simultaneously a representative of the church and an agent of the state. Although today, in the United States, most of the legal aspects of marriage are handled by public officials, in the eighteenth century, the church was responsible for such matters as publishing the banns and issuing a license. Because of the experience of a friend and his own unhappy experience, Wesley was well aware of the complications that can result when the legal aspects of matrimony are mishandled.

Chapter 2 describes the setting for the marriage. An eighteenth-century wedding looked quite different from a big church wedding today, and Wesley's liturgy cannot be properly understood unless those differences are kept in mind. This chapter offers a look at the places where weddings might be held, the people who might be present, the times at which weddings might occur, and Wesley's policy in regard to the place of music in worship. Wedding sermons and nuptial Eucharists are also examined as part of the context within which a marriage takes place.

Wesley's wedding service, like the service in the Book of Common Prayer, lists three purposes for marriage. There was a dispute between Anglican and Puritan theologians over which of those three was most important. This difference of opinion was symptomatic of some strikingly different beliefs regarding the nature of marriage, especially in regard to the question of divorce and remarriage. Furthermore, the Anglicans needed to distinguish their position on the nature of marriage from that of the Roman Catholic Church. There were also those, Wesley among them, who felt that celibacy was preferable to marriage. This belief was seriously challenged by Wesley's relationship with Sophia Hopkey. All these matters are considered in Chapter 3.

Chapter 4 deals with the choice of a marriage partner. How should one choose a spouse? Against a tradition of arranged marriages, what role should one's family play in the choice? How should this be expressed liturgically? And why did Wesley eliminate the giving away of the bride? The chapter ends with a study of the ring ceremony, which originally was part of the ritual at the time a marriage was arranged, and only later made its way into the church service.

Chapter 5 deals with married life as expressed in the wedding vows and the prayers offered for the couple. What was Wesley's understanding of married life? What are the responsibilities undertaken by husbands and wives when they marry? Some of Wesley's family members had entered miserably unhappy marriages. How did Wesley respond to this and how did his beliefs about married life affect his relationship with his own wife?

The conclusion summarizes the major findings of this study and spells out their implications for the ministry of the contemporary church. The complete text of Wesley's wedding service and the prayer book service from which it was drawn appear in the first appendix.

1

"I Publish the Banns of Marriage"

Marriage Law

Private Marriage Contracts

W<small>E</small> turn our attention first to the laws concerning marriage that were in effect in England during Wesley's lifetime. Much of this legislation was concerned with controlling the problems created by clandestine marriages. Although many people did not realize it, during the first fifty years of Wesley's life a legal English marriage could be contracted privately between a man and a woman without any written documentation, without witnesses, and without a religious ceremony of any kind.[1] In order to understand this, we need to review briefly some of the history of wedding customs in previous centuries.

In the late Middle Ages, the marriage was preceded by the "espousals," a formal promise to marry which may be given months or even years before the marriage itself. The espousals typically consisted of the verbal expression of consent to marry one another, the presentation of gifts, called *sponsalia*, the giving and receiving of a ring, a kiss, the joining of hands, and, for persons of property, the settling of a dowry in writing.[2] Couples who had promised themselves to each other in such a manner, spoke of one another as "husband" and "wyf" from then on.[3] Intercourse or even cohabitation was common among espoused couples,[4] although chastity was the norm among the propertied classes of Wesley's era.[5] Before the birth of their first child, the couple went to the church for a formal marriage.[6] The marriage took place *in facie ecclesiae,* that is, at the doors of the church. A nuptial mass might follow inside the church itself.[7] As can be seen from this account, persons were, in effect, bound to each other in marriage from the time of the espousals; the later ceremony *in facie ecclesiae* was largely a formality.

15

This system was, of course, open to many abuses. Young persons faced with the prospect of being forced by their families into a marriage they did not want could secretly espouse themselves to someone else. Likewise, people seeking to be released from an unhappy marriage in an age when legal divorce was impossible could claim to have contracted marriage with someone else before entering the present union, thus rendering their current marriage null and void.[8]

The Council of Trent sought to put an end to such abuses by prohibiting future clandestine marriages, although previously contracted unions would continue to be recognized. Trent required that all marriages must be preceded by three public announcements of the forthcoming nuptials. A priest and two witnesses must be present at the wedding, and the marriage must be recorded in the parish register.[9] But in England, popes and councils no longer had any power, so clandestine marriages there continued to be legally binding through the first half of the eighteenth century.

Eighteenth-century English law differentiated between two types of marriage contracts: spousals *de futuro* and spousals *de praesenti*.

> Spousals *de futuro* are a mutual promise or covenant of marriage to be had afterwards; as when the man saith to the woman, I will take thee to my wife, and she then answereth, I will take thee to my husband. Spousals *de praesenti* are a mutual promise or contract of present matrimony: as when the man doth say to the woman, I do take thee to my wife, and she then answereth, I do take thee to my husband.[10]

A contract *de futuro*, if not followed by consummation (which implied *present* consent and therefore rendered the contract binding for life), could be broken by mutual consent.[11] But a contract *de praesenti* was quite a different matter. The standard text on marriage contracts in the first half of the eighteenth century in England was Henry Swinburne's *A Treatise of Spousals*. Swinburne's treatise explained the significance of *de praesenti* contracts.

> . . . there is no difference in Substance betwixt *Spousals de praesenti* (which make up a principal part of this Book) and *Matrimony*, only the Publick Office, and the greater Solemnity of the Act, together with the Benediction of the Minister, are by Law requisite to compleat the Matrimony, before it be capable of those Legal Effects of Dower and Legitimation of Issue. . . .

. . . that woman, and that man, which have contracted Spousals *de praesenti;* as, *(I do take thee to my Wife)* and *(I do take thee to my Husband)* cannot by any Agreement dissolve those Spousals, but are reputed for very Husband and Wife in respect of the Substance and indissoluble Knot of Matrimony . . .[12]

We find substantially the same position stated by another expert on English law writing in 1732.

By the canon law, as it is received in England, and become part of the laws of the realm, a contract in words of the present time, seriously and solemnly made, is, in truth and substance, matrimony indissoluble. It has been the general opinion of learned divines and lawyers, that, *tho, there should be no evidence, according to the rules of the law, of such spousals,* the parties having really, tho' secretly, contracted themselves, yet they are thereby become so far man and wife before God, that neither can, with a safe and good conscience, marry elsewhere, so long as the other party liveth.[13]

But even contracts *de praesenti* could be rendered invalid in some cases. If, for example, either party attached certain conditions to the contract, the entire agreement could be nullified. Henry Swinburne wrote, "In some cases the conditional contract is reputed simple [that is, uncomplicated by conditions] and hath its present force, as if no condition had been expressed; and in some cases the condition doth utterly destroy the contract."[14] A treatise written in 1732 further explained the law of conditional contracts: "But where the words of the contract are only conditional on one side, and on the other side absolute; or if they are spoken in jest, they are not obligatory." The same writer continues, "In conditional contracts the bond of performance is suspended in the condition, till that be performed, except there follow a relinquishment of it, [i.e., the condition] by copulation of bodies."[15] All of this law regarding private marriage contracts was to be of great personal significance to John Wesley, as we shall see.

The espousals were included as part of the marriage service in the 1549 edition of the Book of Common Prayer. The questions are taken from the medieval Sarum rite (upon which much of the Prayer Book was based), except for the phrase, "after Gods ordeynaunce in the holy estate of matrymonie," which is borrowed from Luther's *Order of Marriage for Common Pastors (nach gottlicher ordenung zum heiligen stande der ehe),*[16] perhaps to emphasize that marriage is an "ordinance," not a "sacrament."[17] In the

1549 Book of Common Prayer the questions are worded in the future tense: "Wilt thou haue thys woman . . ." and "Wilt thou haue thys man . . ."; and in each case the answer is, "I will." Except for changes in spelling and punctuation and replacing the word "to" with "unto" and "you" with "ye," the 1662 version of the espousals is exactly the same as the 1549 text.[18] It was these espousals that Wesley retained in the *Sunday Service* with only a minor change in the wording.[19]

Banns and Licenses

The Council of Trent had tried to combat clandestine marriages by requiring, among other things, that the forthcoming marriage be publicly announced three times prior to the wedding (see page 16). Although clandestine marriages continued to be recognized in England until 1754, all editions of the Book of Common Prayer required three readings of the banns before a church wedding could be performed.

The word "banns" seems to be derived from the feudal method of summoning an army, *bannire in hostem.*

> The raising of the king's banner marked the place of assembly, and the primitive meaning of *bannire* was, to call the people to the *bann,* or standard. The term was then applied to summoning on any other public occasion, and thence to any proclamation.[20]

One such purpose for a public gathering would be to hear a proclamation regarding outlaws and traitors, and thus the verb "to ban" came to mean "to prohibit or condemn."[21] The first English reference to banns in connection with marriage is Canon 11 of the Synod of Westminster from the year 1200. The medieval rubrics specified that the banns were to be announced at mass "when the greater number of people should be present."[22]

The 1549 Book of Common Prayer stated that "the bannes must be asked three seueral Sondayes or holy daies, in the seruice time, the people being present, after the accustomed manner." A further rubric required that if the persons to be married lived in separate parishes, the curate who was to officiate at the ceremony must have a certificate from the curate of the other parish confirming that the banns had been announced three times in that parish as well.[23]

The 1662 prayer book added greater specificity to these instructions. The curate was to announce the banns "after the accustomed manner" in these words: "I publish the Banns of Marriage between M. of _____ and N. of _____. If any of you know cause, of just impediment, why these two persons should not be joyned together in holy Matrimony, ye are to declare it: This is the first (second, or third) time of asking." The 1662 prayer book also specified that the banns were to be read "immediately before the Sentences for the Offertory."[24]

But bishops had the authority to issue licenses permitting marriage without the reading of banns. These licenses stated where the marriage was to take place and the hours between which it may occur. The Archbishop of Canterbury could issue special licenses permitting marriage at "any convenient time or place." Banns and licenses were both valid for a period of three months.[25]

By the seventeenth century, nearly all the well-to-do were evading the banns by obtaining licenses. One early eighteenth-century observer described the situation in this way:

> To proclaim Banns is a Thing no Body now dares to have done; very few are willing to have their Affairs declar'd to all the World in a Publick Place, when for a Guinea they may do it *snug* and without Noise; and my good friends the Clergy, who find their Accounts in it, are not very Zealous to prevent it. Thus then, they by what they call *Licence* are marry'd in their Closets, in the Presence of a couple of Friends that serve as Witnesses.[26]

On the other hand, in certain localities, it was very easy for anyone to be married quickly and inexpensively without either banns or a license. In districts which lay outside immediate ecclesiastical supervision, unscrupulous clergy carried on a brisk trade performing legally recorded marriages for a fee with no questions asked. One church register shows that some forty thousand marriages took place there between 1664 and 1691, an average of four weddings a day, every day of the week for twenty-seven years![27] A certain chapel advertised a wedding fee of five shillings, but would dispense with the fee if the couple agreed to hold their wedding dinner there.[28]

But the most notorious wedding trade was in the Fleet district of London, particularly between 1700 and 1750. Fleet weddings were legally valid and properly recorded, but cheap.[29] Fleet marriages began in the chapel of the Fleet Prison[30] where clerical prisoners were detained in their cells only at night. While imprisoned from 1709 to 1740 one John Gainham, nicknamed the "Bishop of Hell," married thirty-six thousand couples.[31] Fleet clergymen would, for a fee, fraudulently date a marriage registration to legitimize children already born, or even supply a husband for a woman who was eager to marry. Fleet notice boards advertised "Marriages performed within," and hawkers stopped passersby and asked, "Sir, would you be pleased to walk in and be married?"[32]

Legislation was passed in an effort to put an end to such operations. Beginning in 1694, any priest who married a couple without a license or the reading of banns was subject to a fine of one hundred pounds.[33] Legislation enacted in 1712 provided that half the fine collected from a priest convicted of marrying a couple without a license or the reading of banns be paid to the informer![34] But despite these efforts, the Fleet wedding trade continued at a brisk pace until it was finally halted by the Marriage Act of 1753.

Marriage law in the American colonies was, of course, based on that of the mother country. All the colonies required either the reading of banns or, in some places, the posting of a public notice announcing one's intention to marry. In lieu of banns or a public notice, a license could be obtained in most of the colonies from the governor or the county court. Persons contracting marriage without banns or a license were subject to a fine or other penalties, but only in New York were such marriages declared null and void.[35]

During his tenure in Georgia, John Wesley had adhered strictly to the rubric concerning the banns, and it was exasperating for him that so many of his fellow clerics did not do the same. His annoyance is clear in this entry he made in his diary for 6 September 1736.

> Many complaints being made of what had been done in my absence by Mr. Dyson, Chaplain of the Independent Company, who had now been at Savannah several weeks, I went to his lodgings, and taxed him, (1) with baptizing several strong, healthy children in private houses, which was what I had entirely broken through; (2) with marrying several couples without first publishing the banns, which he knew was contrary to the rubric and canon both; and (3) with endeavouring to make a division between my parishioners and me, by speaking against me before them, both as to my life and preaching. The two last charges he denied, but owned the first, promised never to do it again, and did the very same thing the next day. O discipline! Where art thou to be found? Not in England, or (as yet) in America.[36]

While in Savannah, Wesley had a chronic problem with a minister in nearby South Carolina who had married a number of Wesley's parishioners without either banns or a license. Wesley's toleration of this impropriety was pushed beyond the limit when, on 12 March 1737, this man presided at the hastily arranged marriage of Sophia Hopkey, with whom John Wesley himself was deeply in love. Exactly a month later, on 12 April, Wesley decided to take action.

> Being determined, if it were possible, to put a stop to one of my neighbors of Carolina, who had married several of my parishioners without either banns or license, and, as I was informed, designed to do so still, I set out for Charleston in a sloop. . . . I went to Mr. Garden, the minister of Charleston and Commissary for the Bishop of London, and related Mr. Ch[iffelle]'s behaviour to him. He assured me, he would effectually prevent anything of that kind for the future, said that he believed no other clergyman in the province would be guilty of such irregularity, but that, however, he would caution them against it at the General Meeting of the clergy, which was to be the week following.[37]

Wesley remained in Charleston for the meeting of the clergy, where he received the assurances he was seeking. On 22 April, he wrote in his diary, "I met the clergy of the province at Mr. Garden's, who severally assured me they would never interfere with me in anything, nor (in particular) marry any persons of our province without a letter from me desiring them so to do."[38]

As was customary for persons of his social class, John Wesley's brother Charles obtained a license prior to his marriage rather than having the banns read three times in public worship. His journal reveals that he obtained the license two days prior to his marriage, and the bishop's surrogate, Mr. Williams, was "extremely civil" and refused to accept his customary fee from a brother clergyman.[39]

There is no clear indication whether John Wesley, at the time of his own marriage, submitted to the reading of the banns or obtained a license. It would be customary for a person of his social class to obtain a license, but we have no record of his having done so. His journal reveals that on Saturday, 2 February 1751, Wesley decided he would marry Molly Vazeille. The marriage took place either on Monday, 18 February or Tuesday, 19 February.[40] Since there were three Sundays between Wesley's decision to marry and the date of the marriage itself (3, 10, and 17 February), it would have been possible for the banns to be published three times before the marriage took place. In light of his own statements in his Georgia diaries, it would be highly out of character for John Wesley to marry without either banns or a license.

However, given the lack of any documentary evidence in favor of either banns or a license, we must conclude that the social customs of the day strongly favor John Wesley's having obtained a license.

In the *Sunday Service*, Wesley retained the prayer book rubric regarding the banns, but with certain alterations because of the radical difference in social conditions between England and America. As James White points out, "His book was intended for itinerant preachers in the process of gathering congregations rather than for established clergy in parish churches."[41] Therefore, the *Sunday Service* requires that the banns be published "in the Congregation," rather than "in the Church." The option of publishing the banns on "Holy-dayes" [*sic*] as well as Sundays is eliminated, since Wesley had already explained in his introduction to the *Sunday Service*, "Most of the holy-days (so called) are omitted, as at present answering no valuable end."[42] Wesley allows further flexibility by requiring only that the banns be published "in the Time of Divine Service," rather than the prayer book's more specific "immediately before the sentences for the Offertory." Also, the word "Curate" is replaced throughout the *Sunday Service* with "Minister,"[43] a more general term appropriate for the flexible situation of American Methodism. The formula to be repeated in publishing the banns is unchanged, but the rubric concerning persons from different parishes is eliminated. Since Methodists were a small minority of the American population, and a Methodist might well marry someone who was not a member of a Methodist congregation, such a requirement could hardly be enforced.

Impediments to Marriage

Near the beginning of the marriage service in the prayer book, there is a sentence that is familiar even to those whose contact with the church is minimal: "Therefore, if any man can shew any just cause why they may not lawfully be joyned together, let him now speak, or else hereafter for ever hold his peace." The text is from the medieval Sarum rite, except for the last phrase, which comes from Luther *("oder shweige darnach")*. This is followed immediately by a strongly worded charge to the couple.

> I require and charge you both (as ye will answer at the dreadfull day of Judgement, when the secrets of all hearts shall be disclosed), that if either of you know any impediment, why ye may not be lawfully

joyned together in Matrimony, ye do now confess it; For be ye well assured, that so many as are coupled together otherwise than Gods [sic] word doth allow, are not joyned together by God, neither is their Matrimony lawfull.

The source of this statement is the medieval York rite, which, even prior to the Reformation, addressed this statement to the couple in English rather than Latin. Except for changing "ye" to "you," Wesley retained both the statement to the congregation and the statement to the couple in the *Sunday Service.*[44]

These statements, which amount to a fourth and a fifth publication of the banns, call for the declaration of any "just cause" which would prevent this couple from being "lawfully joyned together in Matrimony." Three impediments were specifically identified in English law of this period: a previous marriage still in existence, kinship within certain prohibited degrees, and the lack of parental consent for persons under the age of twenty-one.[45] Leaving the matter of parental consent for a detailed discussion in chapter 4, we turn our attention now to the impediments of polygamy and consanguinity.

Polygamy was not uncommon in eighteenth-century England, especially among the lower classes who made up such a large proportion of the Methodist societies. Because on the one hand it was easy to be married without either banns or a license and on the other hand a legal divorce was not possible, a person might simply abandon one spouse and marry someone else.

A case in point is that of Sarah Ryan, whom Wesley appointed as housekeeper of the Kingswood school in 1757. At the age of nineteen, she had married a man whom she later discovered to have been already married. He eventually deserted her. She then married an Irish sailor who also left her. This was followed by yet another marriage to an Italian sailor with whom she lived until the Irishman returned and claimed her again as *his* wife! She moved in again with the Irishman, despite his ill-treatment of her, and lived with him until he abandoned her once again. At the age of thirty she was converted as a result of Wesley's preaching. Three years later, he appointed her to her position at Kingswood.[46]

Wesley's appointment of Sarah Ryan to such a position generated much criticism, especially from his wife. For instance, there was the time that Sarah Ryan was presiding at a dinner for Wesley and sixty or seventy Methodist preachers. When Mrs. Wesley entered the room and saw her there, she shouted out to the whole company, "The whore now serving you has three husbands living!"[47]

But despite his compassion for Sarah Ryan, John Wesley was opposed to the practice of marrying another person while one's first spouse was still alive. This is particularly clear in his comments on biblical texts dealing with polygamy. For example, Wesley does not hesitate to call Jacob's marriage to both Leah and Rachel a sin, even though it came about as a result of Laban's trickery.

> Hereby he drew *Jacob* into the sin and snare, and disquiet of multiplying wives. *Jacob* did not design it, but to have kept as true to *Rachel* as his father had done to *Rebekah;* he that had lived without a wife to the eighty fourth year of his age could then have been very well content with one: but *Laban,* to dispose of his two daughters without portions, and to get seven years service more out of *Jacob,* thus imposeth upon him, and draws him into such a strait, that he had some colourable reason for marrying them both.[48]

Commenting upon the shortage of wives for the tribe of Benjamin reported in Judges 21, Wesley had this to say:

> . . . we may see, they had no very favourable opinion of *polygamy,* because they did not allow it in this case, when it might seem most necessary for the reparation of a lost tribe.[49]

Jesus' statement in Mark 10:11, "Whosoever shall put away his wife, and marry another, committeth adultery against her," is the basis for Wesley's conclusion, "All polygamy is here totally condemned."[50] And when Paul writes in 1 Corinthians 7:2, "Nevertheless, to avoid fornication, let every man have his own wife," Wesley emphasizes the words, "his own," and comments, "For Christianity allows no polygamy."[51] For Wesley, monogamy was the only permissible form of marriage for a Christian. "I totally deny," he wrote in a letter, "that supposed matter of fact that polygamy was allowed among the primitive Christians or that the converts 'who had many wives were not required to put any of them away.'"[52]

But if Wesley took a strong stand against polygamy, his position on marriage between kindred was somewhat more lenient than the official teaching of the Anglican Church which can be traced to Archbishop Matthew Parker. In 1563, Archbishop of Canterbury Parker had written an "Admonition" against clandestine marriages, remarriage after divorce, and marriage within prohibited degrees of kinship. Appended to the "Admonition" was a table identifying sixty forms of consanguinity that would preclude marriage between the related persons. Parker based his table on the incest laws in Leviticus 18, but he expanded upon Leviticus by treating the sexes equally.[53] For example, since Leviticus specifically states that a man may not marry his granddaughter (Leviticus 18:10), Parker concluded that neither may a woman marry her grandson. Parker also argued that since husband and wife are one flesh, a relationship by marriage was as much an impediment to matrimony as relationship by blood.[54] Thus, a woman may not marry her nephew, even if he is the son of her dead husband's sister and there is no blood relationship between them.

Parker's table of forbidden degrees was officially accepted by Canon 99 in 1603. After that, it was routinely printed in the Prayer Book, along with the Thirty-nine Articles of Religion.[55] All marriages contrary to Parker's table were considered "incestuous and unlawful, and consequently shall be dissolved as void from the beginning."[56]

But in 1756 a contrary opinion was expressed in a work written by a man named John Fry. Wesley read Fry's work the same year it was published, and he was favorably impressed by it.

I read over Mr. Fry's *Case of Marriage between Near Relations Considered.* It is the best tract I ever read upon the subject; I suppose the best that is extant. And two points, I think, he has fully proved: (1) that many marriages commonly supposed to be unlawful are neither contrary to the law of nature, nor the revealed law of God, nor the law of the land; (2) that Ecclesiastical Courts have no right to meddle with any case of this kind.[57]

Twenty-nine years later, Wesley again read Fry's tract, and again he remarked on it in his journal.

This week I read over again, and carefully considered, Mr. Fry's tract upon Marriage. I wonder it is not more known, as there is nothing on the head like it in the English tongue. I still think he has proved, to a demonstration, that no marriages are forbidden either by the law of God or of England but those of brothers and sisters, and those in the ascending and descending line. The contrary supposition seems to be built wholly in a misinterpretation of that expression in Lev. xviii, "Thou shalt not uncover her nakedness." But this, he clearly shows, does not mean to *marry* a woman, but to *deflower* her.[58]

Wesley did not include Parker's "Table of Kindred and Affinity," in the *Sunday Service.*[59]

The prayer book required that anyone who interrupted the marriage service with an alleged impediment must be able to offer some proof in support of the charges and must be willing to deposit a substantial sum of money as a guarantee. If the interrupter could not do this, then the service must continue.[60] Wesley omitted all of this from the *Sunday Service,* since the judicial function of the Anglican priest was not a role inherited by Methodist preachers in America. But the following rubric, which began, "If no impediment be alledged," and which Wesley retained, allows for the possibility that the service might be halted at this point if, in the opinion of the minister, an allegation of sufficient merit is brought forth.

The Marriage Act of 1753

In 1753 Parliament passed a new Marriage Act "for the better preventing of clandestine marriages." This new legislation radically altered the way marriages were contracted in England. Private marriage contracts would no longer be recognized. This act required that all marriages take place in the parish church of one of the parties. Only the Archbishop of Canterbury could grant dispensations from this requirement.[61] The marriage must be recorded in the parish register and signed by both parties.[62] The witnesses were also required to sign the register.[63] No person under the age of twenty-one could be married if a parent or guardian objected after the publication of the banns, nor could anyone under twenty-one evade the banns by obtaining a license without parental consent.[64] If no morning service was held on a given Sunday, then the banns could be read at the evening service.[65] Even marriages performed by clergy were invalid if they failed to meet the legal requirements.[66]

The Marriage Act did not apply to royalty, Quakers, Jews, or to those married overseas,[67] but it did apply to Roman Catholics. After the law went into effect, English Catholics desiring to marry would ask a Catholic priest to bless their marriage at home first, then they went to the local Anglican Church for the legal ceremony.[68]

Other segments of the population found their own ways of adapting to these new legal requirements. One source records, "On March 25, 1754, the last day before the Act came into operation, no fewer than two hundred and seventeen marriages were recorded into one Fleet register-book alone."[69] Gretna Green, Scotland, near the English border, became a haven for couples seeking easy marriages in the second half of the eighteenth century. Scottish law required only a declaration of a couple's intention to marry one another, spoken before witnesses.[70] A visitor to South Wales in the 1760s found that the miners of that region had found their own way of coping with the new marriage law.

> Some Couples (especially among the miners) either having no friends, or seeing this kind of public marriage too troublesome and Impracticable, procure a man to wed them privately which will not cost above two or 3 mugs of ale. Sometimes half a dozen Couples will agree to a merry meeting, and are thus wedded and bedded together. This they call *Priodas vach* (i.e. the Little wedding) and is frequently made use of among miners and others to make sure of a woman. . . . The little wedding doth not bind them so Effectually, but that after a months trial they may part by Consent, when the Miner leaves his Mistress, and removes to a Minework in some distant Country, and the Girl is not worse look'd upon among the miners than if she had been an unspotted virgin, so Prevalent and Arbitrary is Custom.[71]

Even though an edition of the *Sunday Service* was published in 1786 for the use of British Methodists, it is doubtful if the marriage service from that book was ever used, because since 1753 only priests of the Church of England were legally authorized to preside at a marriage. But in the United States, no such problem existed. Virginia in 1784 and Georgia in 1785 were the last two states to pass statutes permitting clergy of all denominations to officiate at legal marriages.[72] The early *Disciplines* of the Methodist Episcopal Church permit ordained deacons and elders "to perform the office of matrimony," but not lay preachers.[73]

Case Histories

John Goole and Margaret Hudson

We are now in a position to see what effect all these civil and ecclesiastical regulations concerning marriage had upon the life of John Wesley.

The first such case in which John Wesley is known to have been involved concerned a young man named John Boyce who in 1727 at the age of sixteen, matriculated at Christ Church, Oxford, and became one of Charles Wesley's students. Boyce was the son of Sir John Boyce, who was three times mayor of Oxford. During his time as an undergraduate at Oxford, young Mr. Boyce met and fell in love with Margaret Hudson, a girl his own age. But Margaret's mother disapproved of their relationship, and they stopped seeing each other early in the year 1730.[74]

Around Easter 1730 Margaret began to be courted by the Reverend John Goole, a forty-year-old widower who had been vicar of the parish church that Margaret and her family attended. At first, Margaret was receptive to his advances, although later she was cooler toward him. But on 10 June 1731 they entered a "most binding and serious engagement," using the office of matrimony in the Book of Common Prayer. They decided to defer the public ceremony until Margaret was twenty-one. Apparently neither of them realized that by making a marriage covenant in the words of the present tense, they had bound themselves to each other in a legal marriage.

But the following month, Margaret's mother and John Boyce's father allowed John and Margaret to be reunited after an absence of sixteen months. Their love was rekindled, and they were married on 29 July 1731. John Wesley, who was aware of Margaret's marriage contract with John Goole, recorded in his diary for that day, "Mr. B. married Mr. G's wife."

John Goole, who had been out of town at the time of Margaret's wedding, at first refused to believe that his betrothed had married somebody else. But when he realized that the awful news was true, he sued Boyce and his wife for damages of three thousand pounds. In November 1731 he was awarded two hundred pounds damages by the Court of Common Pleas in compensation for the trousseau he had purchased for Margaret.

In the meantime, Goole became aware of Henry Swinburne's *Treatise of Spousals,* which made him realize that he and Margaret had entered a legally binding marriage when they formed their *de praesenti* contract. This caused him to feel that he had not only a legal right, but a moral duty to separate Margaret and the man she had illegally married.

Before proceeding further, Goole sought expert legal advice. He consulted a local barrister who suggested asking the opinion of two legal experts in London. John Wesley became the envoy who traveled to London, obtained the opinions, and carried them back to Oxford. Both opinions strongly supported Goole's position. Margaret's *de praesenti* contract with Goole was binding, despite her being a minor. Goole did not have the power to release her from the contract, and her later marriage to John Boyce was null and void, according to these legal authorities.

These opinions were shown to both Boyce and Goole in a meeting at which John Wesley was also present. Boyce at first offered not to live with Margaret until the case was settled, but he later changed his mind, perhaps because Margaret was pregnant at the time. Goole pursued the matter to the highest level, the Court of Arches, an ecclesiastical court of appeal, but by the time the case finally came to trial in June 1733, it was nearly time for Margaret's *second* child to be born. In the meantime, Margaret's lawyers had discovered that portion of Swinburne's *Treatise of Spousals* which explains that, even in contracts *de praesenti*, "when these words of the present time are uttered in *jeast* or *sport* . . . such wanton words are not at all obligatory in so serious a matter as is matrimony." Margaret told the court that she had not been serious when she entered her marriage contract with Goole and the court believed her. Their final judgment was that the "pretended marriage contract" between Margaret and Goole "was and is null and void and altogether invalid in law."

The case of John Goole demonstrates the futility of one party trying to enforce a private marriage contract after the other party has decided to marry somebody else. It was a lesson that John Wesley, though an observer in this case, would later have occasion to apply in a more personal context. For Wesley himself was to become involved in another complicated situation regarding a private marriage contract that would affect him far more powerfully than did this matter between John Goole and Margaret Hudson. That situation was his own private marriage contract with a young woman named Grace Murray.

John Wesley and Grace Murray

In August 1748 Wesley became ill and was confined to his home at Newcastle. He was nursed back to health by Grace Murray, a thirty-two-year-old widow whom Wesley had hired as his housekeeper. Her constant attention during his illness caused Wesley to notice and appreciate her more and more. One day he startled her by saying, "If ever I marry, I think you will be the person." Grace responded with amazement, "This is too great a Blessing for me: I can't tell how to believe it. This is all I could have wished for under Heaven, if I had dared to wish for it."[75]

They spoke of marriage, but it is not clear whether or not they entered any formal marriage contract at this time. At one place in his diary, Wesley says that Grace Murray "consented to my proposal at Newcastle." But in describing their relationship in a letter, he wrote, "There was no so Explicit an Engagement as would stand good in Law: But such an one there was, as ought in conscience to have prevented any other, till it should be dissolved."

When Wesley's health was recovered, he and Grace traveled together for two weeks through Yorkshire and Derbyshire. Wesley recorded that "she was unspeakably useful both to me and to the Societies." He left her at the home of his friend and fellow preacher, John Bennet, and traveled on alone.

Wesley apparently did not yet realize that Bennet had also been seeking Grace's hand in marriage since the time she had cared for *him* when *he* was seriously ill two years previously. Shortly after Wesley left, Bennet again asked Grace to marry him, and a day or two later, she accepted! Bennet, evidently aware of her close relationship with Wesley, asked, "Is there not a Contract between you and Mr. Wesley?" She replied, "There is not." They each wrote a letter to John Wesley in which they expressed their desire to marry each other. Grace wrote in her letter that "she believed it was the will of God."

But over the following months, Grace found that she was utterly unable to choose between her two suitors. Wesley recorded in his diary, "When she received a Letter from me, she resolved to live and die with me, and wrote to me just what she felt. When she heard from him, her Affection for him revived, and she wrote to him in the tenderest manner."

In February 1749 she wrote to Bennet that if he loved her, he should meet her at Sheffield because she would soon be leaving for Ireland. Bennet intended to come, but the death of his brother-in-law detained him. When Bennet did not appear at Sheffield, Grace went to John Wesley in Bristol. There they talked about all that had happened. Grace believed herself bound by her *de futuro* marriage contract with Bennet, but Wesley persuaded her that her prior commitment was to him.

For several months, during which time Grace had no contact with John Bennet at all, she traveled with Wesley in Ireland. Their relationship grew steadily stronger, and before leaving Dublin, they committed themselves to one another in a marriage contract *de praesenti*.

But upon their return to England, Grace heard some gossip about John Wesley and another woman. In jealousy, she impulsively wrote a loving letter to John Bennet. By the next day, she regretted what she had done, but the letter had already been sent. When Bennet received it, he was encouraged to renew his quest of Grace Murray.

Bennet met Wesley and Grace at Epworth on 30 August 1749.

The two men talked frankly, and Bennet was able to persuade Wesley that his own claim to Grace Murray's hand was stronger than Wesley's. The next morning, Wesley sent Grace a message that they should not see each other again.

Upon receiving this message, Grace ran to Wesley in great distress and begged him not to say such things. But when Bennet appeared and asserted his right to her, Wesley decided that rather than putting all of them through the turmoil of a protracted struggle, the more loving thing to do in this case was to step aside.

That afternoon, Wesley received word that Grace Murray had suddenly become very ill. When Wesley came to see her, she asked him, "How can you possibly think that I love any other better than you? I love you a thousand times better than ever I loved John Bennet in my Life. But I do not know what to do. I am afraid if I don't marry him, he will run mad."

But that night, Bennet and another preacher came to visit Grace. They told her they would not leave until she gave them the answer they were seeking. At last she said that she would, indeed, marry John Bennet.

When Wesley heard about this, he was more confused than ever. For several days he was unsure what he ought to do. On 6 September he asked her directly to choose between him and Bennet. She replied over and over again, "I am determined by conscience, as well as inclination, to live and die with you."

Wesley then wrote Bennet a letter in which he rebuked his fellow preacher for the way he had conducted himself, and concluded, "You may tear her away by violence. But my Consent I cannot, dare not give: Nor I fear can God give you his Blessing." But the letter went astray and was never delivered. Grace also voluntarily wrote a letter to Bennet in which she stated that it had been wrong for them to enter any marriage agreement without first consulting Mr. Wesley.

Having settled it in her mind that it was Wesley she wanted to marry, Grace wanted them to marry at once, but Wesley insisted that three things needed to happen first. The conflict with John Bennet must be resolved, Charles Wesley must give his consent (since the brothers had an agreement that neither of them would marry without the other's consent), and the Methodist Societies must be notified of Wesley's intention to marry. Grace said that she would not be willing to wait longer than a year for these things to happen. Wesley replied, "Perhaps less time will suffice."

During the next few days, Grace told Wesley several times, "In times past I could have married another, if you would have given me away. But now it is impossible we should part: God has united us forever." One of the preachers, Christopher Hopper, who was familiar with John Bennet's relationship with Grace Murray, agreed to intervene with Bennet on Wesley's behalf. At Grace Murray's request, she and Wesley renewed their *de praesenti* marriage contract, with Christopher Hopper as a witness. Noticing that Grace seemed to pause and tremble before saying the words of the contract, Hopper asked her, "Sister Murray, have you any scruple upon your mind?" Wesley added, "If you have the least scruple, I beg you would stop. Pray do." She replied, "I have none at all," and she spoke the words of the contract. Four days later, Grace wrote a letter in which she said, "If Mr. Bennet comes to Newcastle, write to me immediately; for I must not see him. It will tear my soul to pieces: Seeing I can by no means help him now. For whom God hath joined together, no man can put asunder."

Wesley and Grace parted an hour after renewing their marriage contract. Two nights after leaving, he had a disturbing dream about Grace and John Bennet. He awoke from the dream and was unable to sleep any more that night. The next day, he began a letter to her by expressing his fear that they would never meet again. That Sunday the Old Testament lesson happened to be taken from Ezekiel 24:15–17, "Son of Man, behold I take from thee the desire of thine eyes with a stroke." These words affected Wesley so powerfully that within moments he was feeling quite ill.

Charles Wesley was shocked to hear that his brother intended to marry a household servant, and he was even more shocked to hear that his brother's prospective bride had previously agreed to marry John Bennet. Charles feared a terrible scandal would result from all of this, and the work of the Methodist Societies could be seriously damaged or even destroyed. On Monday, 25 September, Charles found his brother and warned him of the results that he feared would come about if John went ahead with his marriage plans. A heated argument followed. John preached on the following morning, and when he returned to the house that afternoon, his brother had already left.

Grace Murray was staying at this time with a woman named Hannah Broadwood. Wesley was scheduled to preach in that town the next day, so he mounted his horse and rode to the Broadwoods' home. But when he arrived, he was told that Charles had been there and had left with Grace Murray two hours previously. James Broadwood volunteered to pursue them and, if possible, bring Grace Murray back.

The next day, 28 September, Wesley set aside for fasting and prayer. The following Sunday, he wrote in his diary, "I was in great heaviness, my Heart was sinking in me like a Stone. Only so long as I was preaching I felt ease. When I had done, the weight returned." That night, he had a dream that he saw Grace Murray executed by hanging. Monday he again spent in fasting and prayer.

On Monday evening, he received a letter from George Whitefield, urging him to come to Leeds to meet with Charles Wesley and Whitefield on Wednesday evening. But when Wesley arrived, Whitefield told him that Charles would not come until John Bennet and Grace Murray were married. Whitefield insisted that, in his judgment, Grace Murray was Wesley's wife, and that he had said so to John Bennet, but to no avail.

About eight o'clock Thursday morning Wesley received word that John Bennet and Grace Murray had been married on Tuesday. What happened next, we will let Wesley tell in his own words.

> My Brother came an hour after. I felt no Anger. Yet I did not desire to see him. But Mr. Whitefield constrained me. After a few Words had past, He accosted me with, " . . . I renounce all intercourse with you, but what I would have with an heathen man or a publican." I felt no Emotion. It was only adding a drop of water to a drowning man. Yet I calmly accepted his Renunciation and acquiesced therein. Poor Mr. Whitefield and John Nelson burst into Tears. They prayed, cried, and intreated, till the Storm past away. We could not speak, but only fell on each other's neck.
>
> John Bennet then came in. Neither of us could speak. But we kist each other and wept.

Later, Wesley was able to reconstruct what had happened in the past few days. Charles Wesley had gone to Grace Murray and warned her that a great scandal would ensue if she married John Wesley after having already promised herself to John Bennet. She left with Charles, believing that he was taking her to meet with both John Bennet and John Wesley, and that John Wesley had arranged the whole thing. Hearing that John Bennet was at Newcastle, Charles arranged for Grace to meet Bennet there. When Grace saw Bennet, she fell at his feet and asked his forgiveness for treating him so poorly. Someone then told her that John Wesley had given her up and would have nothing more to say to her, but he had directed that she be provided a place to stay among the rural Methodist Societies where she might live in obscurity.

Hearing this, someone cried out, "Good God! What will the world say? He is tired of her, and so he thrusts his whore into a corner. Sister Murray, will you consent to this?" She answered, "No, I will die first." Then, turning to Bennet, she said, "I will have John Bennet, if he will have me."

The question as to which of Grace Murray's marriage contracts with Wesley and Bennet should have taken precedence has never been resolved. Even Wesley's own account is self-contradictory at points. In an article entitled "John Wesley's First Marriage," Frank Baker argued that the *de praesenti* contract between Wesley and Grace Murray was a binding agreement which nullified any subsequent marriage to anyone else.[76] Baker was answered by Frederick Maser, who argued in his article "John Wesley's Only Marriage" that the conditions involved in John Wesley's contract with Grace Murray invalidated the contract, so that she was legally free to contract marriage with John Bennet.[77] Wesley clearly regarded Grace as his espoused wife. Sixteen years later, commenting upon the biblical story of David and his promised bride Michal, the daughter of King Saul, Wesley made a comment on the words "my wife" in 2 Samuel 3:14 that sounds strangely personal. *"My wife*—Who, though she was taken from me by force, and constrained to marry another, yet is my rightful wife."[78]

But although he was convinced of the rightness of his cause, Wesley had learned from the case of John Goole the difficulty of winning a legal battle in such a situation, even if he had been willing to put himself and John and Grace Bennet through such an ordeal.

Wesley and Bennet remained on friendly terms for a time, but Bennet left the Methodists in 1752 and became an independent preacher. Grace and John Bennet lived together for ten years and she bore him five children before his death in 1759 at the age of forty-four.[79]

Wesley's last meeting with Grace Bennet took place nearly forty years later, when he was an eighty-five-year-old widower and she was a widow of seventy-two. It is described by Henry Moore, one of Wesley's assistants, who wrote one of the first biographies of John Wesley.

In the year 1788, the son of Mr. Bennet, already mentioned, officiated at a chapel on the pavement in Moorfields, and his mother came to London that year on a visit to him. Mr. Thomas Olivers, having seen her, mentioned the circumstances to Mr. Wesley when I was with him, and intimated that Mrs. Bennet wished to see him. Mr. Wesley, with evident feeling, resolved to visit her; and the next morning he took me with him to Colebrooke-row, where her son then resided. The meeting was affecting; but Mr. Wesley preserved more than his usual self-possession. It was easy to see, notwithstanding the many years which had intervened, that, both in sweetness of spirit and in person and manners, she was a fit subject for the tender regrets expressed in those verses which I have presented to the reader. The interview did not continue long, and I do not remember that I ever heard Mr. Wesley mention her name afterward.[80]

The verses to which Moore refers are a set of thirty-one stanzas which Wesley composed a few days after Grace's marriage to John Bennet. It is fitting that we close this chapter by quoting a portion of that poem.

> O Lord, I bow my sinful Head!
>   Righteous are all thy ways with Man!
> Yet suffer me with Thee to plead,
>   With lowly reverence to complain;
> With deep, unutter'd grief to groan,
> O what is this that Thou hast done!
>
> Oft, as thro' giddy Youth I rov'd,
>   And danc'd along the flowry way
> By Chance or thoughtless Passion mov'd,
>   An easy, unsuspicious Prey
> I fell, while Love's envenom'd Dart
> Thrill'd thro' my Veins, and tore my Heart.
>
> At length, by sad Experience taught,
>   Firm I shook off the abject Yoke;
> Abhor'd his sweetly-poisonous Draught,
>   Thro' all his wily Fetters broke:
> Fixt my Desires on things above,
> And languisht for Celestial Love.
>
> Born on the wings of Sacred Hope
>   Long had I soar'd, and spurn'd the Ground;
> When panting for the Mountain-top
>   My Soul a kindred Spirit found:
> By Heaven intrusted to my Care,
> The Daughter of my Faith and Prayer.
> .   .   .   .
> From Heaven the grateful Ardor came,
>   Pure from the Dross of low Desire:

Well-pleas'd I marked the guiltless Flame,
    Nor dar'd to damp the sacred Fire;
Heaven's Choicest Gift on Man bestow'd,
Strengthning [*sic*] our Hearts and Hands in God.

. . . .

From that glad Hour, with growing Love,
    Heaven's latest, dearest Gift I view'd:
While, pleas'd each Moment to improve,
    We urg'd our way with Strength renew'd,
Our one Desire, our common Aim,
To extol our gracious Master's Name.

Companions now in Weal and Woe,
    No power on Earth could us divide;
Nor Summer's Heat, nor wintry Snow
    Could tear my Partner from my side;
Nor Toil, nor Weariness, nor Pain,
Nor Horrors of the angry Main.

Oft, (tho' as yet the Nuptial Tie
    Was not), clasping her Hand in mine,
What Force, she said, beneath the Sky,
    Can now our well-knit Souls disjoin?
With Thee I'd go to India's Coast,
To Worlds in distant Ocean lost!"

Such was the Friend than Life more dear
    Whom in one luckless baleful Hour,
(For ever mention'd with a Tear)
    The Tempest's unresisted Power,
(O the unutterable Smart!)
Tore from my inly-bleeding Heart.

Unsearchable thy Judgments are,
    O Lord, a bottomless Abyss!
Yet sure thy Love, thy guardian Care,
    O'er all thy Works extended is.
O why didst thou the Blessing send?
Or why thus snatch away my Friend?

What thou hast done I know not now!
    Suffice I shall hereafter know!
Beneath thy chastening Hand I bow:
    That still I live to Thee I owe.
O teach thy deeply-humbled Son
To say, "Father, thy will be done!"

Teach me, from every pleasing Snare
    To keep the Issues of my Heart:
Be thou my Love, my Joy, my Fear!
    Thou my eternal Portion art.
Be thou my never-failing Friend,
And love, O love me to the End![81]

2

"At the Day and Time Appointed"

Time

AFTER the introductory rubrics about the banns, the next rubric in the marriage service from the *Sunday Service* reads, "At the Day and Time appointed for Solemnization of Matrimony, the Persons to be married, standing together, the Man on the Right Hand, and the Woman on the Left, the Minister shall say, . . ."[1] In editions of the prayer book prior to 1662, this rubric had begun with the words, "At the *day* appointed for Solemnization of Matrimony."[2] There was no need to refer to the *time* of the service in earlier editions of the Prayer Book because the *time* was firmly established. Prior to the Reformation, church weddings normally took place on Sunday with the whole parish present.[3] The liturgy consisted of the matrimonial rite itself (which originally took place at the church door), followed by a nuptial mass.[4]

The tradition of Sunday morning weddings was codified by Canon 62 of 1603 which required that church weddings take place between the hours of 8:00 A.M. and noon.[5] The Marriage Act of 1753 perpetuated the same requirement.[6] John Wesley's diaries show that he presided at a number of weddings, all of which took place in the morning, most of them on Sunday.[7]

The medieval Sarum rubrics had prohibited matrimony between the beginning of Advent and the Octave of Epiphany, between Septuagesima and the Octave of Easter, and between Rogation Sunday and the sixth day after Pentecost.[8] This restriction was not included in the Book of Common Prayer, although some felt it should have been. Richard Hooker, a leading Anglican apologist of the late sixteenth century, argued that some seasons of the year are patently unsuitable for the consecration of marriage.

"There is," saith Solomon, "a time for all things, a time to laugh and a time to mourn." That duties belonging unto marriages and offices appertaining to penance are things unsuitable and unfit to be matched together, the Prophets and Apostles themselves do witness. Upon which ground as we might well think it marvellous absurd to see in a church a wedding on the day of a public fast, so likewise in the selfsame consideration our predecessors thought it not amiss to take away the common liberty of marriages during the time which was appointed for the preparation unto and for exercise of general humiliation by fasting and praying, weeping for sins.[9]

A clause which would have reinstated these traditional restrictions regarding the seasons during which weddings may not take place was introduced to the Convocation in 1661, but it never became part of the prayer book.[10] Wesley was apparently not concerned about seasonal restrictions on matrimony, since his diaries show that he presided at weddings during Christmastide, during Lent, and during Rogationtide.[11] Wesley's lack of concern for seasonal restrictions is also reflected in the liturgical calendar he prepared for the *Sunday Service*, in which "Most of the holy-days (so called) are omitted, as at present answering no valuable end."[12]

The fact that the 1662 edition of the prayer book speaks of "the day and *time* appointed for solemnization of Matrimony," indicates that by the middle of the seventeenth century, marriages were no longer routinely taking place at the Sunday morning worship service. As we have already noted, *most* of the weddings at which John Wesley is known to have presided took place on Sunday, but not all. He presided at the Saturday morning wedding of his brother Charles,[13] and he himself was married on either a Monday or a Tuesday.[14] In the *Sunday Service*, Wesley retains the Prayer Book language about "the day and time appointed," without adding any further qualifications.[15]

Nuptial Eucharists

But what of the tradition that the nuptial rite was to be followed by the Eucharist? The 1549 prayer book had required that "The newe maried persones (the same day of their mariage) must receiue the holy communion." But in 1662, this was changed to read, "*It is convenient* that the new married persons should receive the holy Communion at the time of their marriage, *or at the first opportunity after their Marriage.*"[16] And Wesley, in the *Sunday Service*, omitted the rubric about communion altogether![17] Obviously, between 1549 and 1784 there was a significant shift in the Anglican perspective on the relationship between matrimony and the Eucharist. What is the history behind this change in the liturgy?

Although John Calvin specifically prohibited matrimony on eucharistic occasions,[18] the continental reformer Martin Bucer approved the link between matrimony and Eucharist in the 1549 prayer book. He commented, "There is also a very godly ordinance, that the newly wed couple shall also communicate together from the Lord's table: for Christian people ought not to be joined together in matrimony except in Christ the Lord."[19]

Another strong defender of the nuptial Eucharist was Richard Hooker, who spoke of the link between matrimony and Eucharist in his major work, *Of the Laws of Ecclesiastical Polity.* Hooker wrote, "To end the public solemnity of marriage with receiving the blessed Sacrament is a custom so religious and so holy, that if the church of England be blamable in this respect it is not for suffering it to be so much but rather for not providing that it may be more put in ure."[20]

Hooker's spirited defense of the nuptial Eucharist implies that the practice was under attack, as indeed it was. To some Reformed clergy, the practice seemed hopelessly tainted with Romanism.

> Because in Popery no holy action may be done without a mass, they enjoin the new married persons to receive the communion, as they do their Bishops and Priests when they are made.[21]

Even the approval of so notable a reformer as Bucer did not persuade the Dissenters.

> As for the receiving of the Communion when they be married, that it is not to be suffered, unless there be a general receiving, I have before at large declared; and as for the reason that is fathered of M. Bucer, (which is, that those that be Christians may not be joined in marriage but in Christ,) it is very slender and cold; as if the Sacrament of the Supper were instituted to declare any such thing; or they could not declare their joining together in Christ by no means but by receiving the Supper of the Lord.[22]

In 1661, at the Savoy Conference called by Charles II to review and revise the Anglican liturgy, the Presbyterians argued that the rubric requiring communion should be removed from the prayer book.

> This rubric doth either enforce all such as are unfit for the sacrament to forbear Marriage, contrary to scripture, which approves the Mar-

riage of all men; or else compels all that marry to come to the Lord's Table, though never so unprepared; and therefore we desire it may be omitted, the rather because that Marriage-festivals are too often accompanied with such divertisements as are unsuitable to those Christian duties, which ought to be before and follow after the receiving of that holy Sacrament.[23]

The bishops, of course, had a response to these objections.

The rubric enforces none to forbear Marriage, but presumes (as well it may) that all persons marriageable ought to be also fit to receive the holy Sacrament; and Marriage being so solemn a covenant of God, they that undertake it in the fear of God will not stick to seal it by receiving the Holy Communion, and accordingly prepare themselves for it. It were more Christian to desire that those licentious festivities might be suppressed, and the Communion more generally used by those that marry; the happiness would be greater than can easily be expressed.[24]

Francis Procter, in his study of the history of the prayer book, suggests two reasons for the change that took place in the rubric regarding communion in the 1662 prayer book. The first of these is the objection raised by the Presbyterians. This objection undoubtedly had some effect; it is unlikely the rubric would have been changed if nobody had objected to it. But this alone cannot be the whole explanation; the Presbyterians did not receive everything they asked for at the 1661 Savoy Conference. The second reason, which Proctor regards as more probable, is that requiring communion at every marriage raised a problem when the persons to be married were not communicants in the Anglican Church.[25] But Kenneth Stevenson is probably nearer to the heart of the matter when he argues that the change in the 1662 prayer book simply brought the rubric into conformity with actual practice.[26] In most Anglican parishes of this era, the Eucharist was celebrated only three or four times a year.[27] The common acceptance of infrequent celebrations of the Sacrament, combined with the increasing tendency for the matrimonial rite to be observed as an occasional office, and not as part of the Sunday morning liturgy, helped create an environment in which the nuptial Eucharist was likely to be neglected, in spite of the rubric.

It is impossible to tell from the brief entries in his diaries whether John Wesley customarily celebrated Holy Communion at matrimonial services or not. His Sunday weddings were, of course, followed by the Eucharist later in the morning.[28] But whether weddings he performed on other days of the week included a celebration of the Eucharist or not is impossible to say.

Our only detailed account of a marriage at which John Wesley presided is Charles Wesley's description of his own wedding in his *Journal*. In commenting on this occasion, Charles observed, "It was a most solemn season of love! Never had I more of the divine presence at the sacrament."[29] This statement is somewhat ambiguous. Does it mean, "We celebrated the sacrament at my wedding, and never have I experienced more of God's presence at the sacrament than I did on that occasion," or does it mean, "Not even at the sacrament have I experienced more of God's presence than I did at my wedding"? Although the second possibility cannot be ruled out, the evidence favors the first interpretation. In his description of the wedding, Charles comments in sequence upon various aspects of the service, and the reference to the Sacrament comes at a point in the sequence where the Sacrament may well have been celebrated. Thus, the reader is left with the impression that this is another comment upon something that took place at the wedding. Also, Charles was more of a High Churchman than was John, and it is likely he would want the Eucharist celebrated at his wedding.[30] Furthermore, a hymn was sung at Charles's wedding which includes several eucharistic allusions.

> Now the ancient wonder show,
> Manifest thy power below;
> All our thoughts exalt, refine,
> Turn the water into wine.
>
> .   .   .   .
> Raise our hearts to things on high,
> To our Bridegroom in the sky;
> Heaven our hope and highest aim,
> Mystic marriage of the Lamb.
>
> O might each obtain a share
> Of the pure enjoyments there;
> Now, in rapturous surprise,
> Drink the wine of Paradise;
>
> Own, amidst the rich repast,
> Thou hast given the best at last;
> Wine that cheers the host above,
> The best wine of perfect love![31]

In the *Sunday Service* Wesley omitted the rubric regarding communion altogether. James White suggests that this was because of Puritan influence,[32] but there is no evidence that Wesley shared the Puritan objection to nuptial Eucharists. Kenneth Stevenson states that Wesley probably omitted the Eucharist because it was seldom, if ever, celebrated.[33] Stevenson is probably correct about the infrequency of nuptial Eucharists, but he overlooks the fact that Wesley's own practice, which he encouraged the Methodists to follow, was out of step with the prevailing practices of his day. Wesley's admonition to his followers was that they should commune as often as possible.

> If, therefore, we have any regard for the plain command of Christ, if we desire the pardon of our sins, if we wish for strength to believe, to love and obey God, then we should neglect no opportunity of receiving the Lord's Supper; then we must never turn our backs on the feast which our Lord has prepared for us. We must neglect no occasion, which the good providence of God affords us, for this purpose. This is the true rule: So often are we to receive as God gives us opportunity.[34]

Wesley clearly directed that the American Methodist elders were to celebrate the Eucharist every Lord's Day.[35] Why, then, did Wesley remove the rubric concerning matrimonial Eucharists, in spite of his strong insistence upon neglecting no opportunity of receiving the Lord's Supper? Does not the rubric in the prayer book provide an additional opportunity for Christians to receive the Lord's Supper?

Surely both White and Stevenson are partially correct in their explanations. Because weddings were often not held on Sunday, it is probably correct, as Stevenson observes, that the Eucharist was rarely celebrated at matrimonial services. The Puritans had achieved some measure of success in weakening the tie between matrimony and Eucharist. But there is another consideration that must have entered Wesley's thinking, and that pertains to church order.

Wesley recognized, of course, that there was a severe shortage of ordained clergy for the Methodists in North America; he cites this emergency as part of his justification for assuming the power to ordain.[36] But despite this extraordinary step, Wesley consistently maintained that only ordained elders were authorized to administer the Lord's Supper.[37]

The prayer book included the reasonable expectation that most weddings would be performed by priests; therefore, it could en-

courage nuptial Eucharists. But Wesley could make no such as-
sumption regarding the Methodists in America; on the contrary,
he could expect ordained elders to be rather rare among American
Methodists for the foreseeable future. Therefore, because of his
insistence that only ordained elders may administer the Lord's
Supper, and also because nuptial Eucharists were probably even
less common in America than in England, the rubric concerning
communion was deleted.[38]

Place

Wesley's *Sunday Service* is less specific than is the prayer book
regarding where weddings should take place and who should
be present.

As we have seen, the medieval custom was for the marriage to
take place at the front door of the church, followed by a nuptial
mass inside (see page 15). But by 1472 the wedding service sometimes began in the body of the church before the chancel.[39] And
all editions of the prayer book from 1549 through 1662 directed
that at the beginning of the wedding service "the persons to be
married shall come into the body of the church."[40] Wesley, however, deleted the rubric that the service was to take place "in the
body of the church."[41]

When one considers the condition of American Methodist
church architecture at the time, it is easy to understand Wesley's
action. The Methodists in America did have a few substantial
church buildings in 1784, such as Wesley Chapel on John Street
in New York City, St. George's Church in Philadelphia, Lovely
Lane Chapel in Baltimore, and Barratt's Chapel in Delaware.[42] But
a more typical example of American Methodist church architecture of this era would be the "Log Meeting House" built by Robert
Strawbridge in Maryland. This structure was a log cabin twenty-
two feet square with a dirt floor. A large opening in the front wall
constituted the entryway; smaller holes in the walls made the
windows. As was customary in Methodist chapels of that era,
worshipers sat on benches with no backs on them. In 1844, after
this structure was no longer used for worship, it was made into
a barn![43]

Such simple structures as the Log Meeting House were consistent with Wesley's custom of preaching to coal miners and factory
laborers wherever he could gather them, indoors or out. In such
rustic circumstances as the early American Methodists were generally to be found, flexibility regarding liturgical space was essen-

tial. James White observes that throughout the *Sunday Service* "Little is presupposed architecturally. Rubrics about the arrangement of liturgical space are usually eliminated." It is no surprise that Wesley also eliminated all references to clerical garb in the *Sunday Service.*[44]

As for attendance at weddings, the rubric in the prayer book regarding the entrance of the bridal party stated that "the persons to be married shall come into the Body of the Church *with their Friends and Neighbors.*"[45] When marriages were celebrated in conjunction with the Sunday liturgy, a considerable number of people would be present as witnesses. But as Sunday weddings became less common, the attendance at weddings decreased. Indeed, it would be surprising to see a large crowd of people present at a wedding held on a weekday morning.

For example, when John Wesley presided at the wedding of his brother Charles at 8:00 A.M. on Saturday, 8 April 1749, only a handful of people were present. Charles recorded the attendance in his journal: "Her father, sisters, Lady Rudd, Grace Bowen, Betty Williams, and, I think, Billy Tucker, and Mr. James, were all the persons present."[46]

Ten years later, John Wesley noted in his journal the attendance at a wedding in which he had been invited to take part. "I was at a Christian wedding to which were invited only two or three relations, and five clergymen."[47] It was apparently because weddings were increasingly becoming private ceremonies, removed from the context of congregational worship, that Wesley eliminated the reference to "friends and neighbors" in the *Sunday Service.*

But Wesley saw no reason to change the rubric regarding the positioning of the bridal couple so that the man is standing on the right and the woman on the left. This had been the custom since as early as the medieval Sarum Manual, which stated, "The man and the woman should be placed before the door of the church, before God and the priest and the people, the man at the right of the woman, and the woman at the left of the man."[48]

It is possible that marriage services in America were frequently held in private homes rather than in places of public worship.[49] The first American edition of the Book of Common Prayer, published in 1789, states that "the Persons to be married shall come into the body of the Church, *or shall be ready in some proper house.*"[50] Such a setting would only increase the need for flexibility in the requirements regarding liturgical space.

It is somewhat surprising that Wesley eliminated the rubric

that the bridal couple are to kneel for the closing prayers. Wesley elsewhere stated that he himself always knelt for public prayer,[51] and kneeling seems to have been the preferred posture for prayer in early American Methodism.[52] The absence of this rubric is evidently another example of Wesley's efforts to make this service flexible enough to be used in a variety of settings.

Wedding Sermons

Just before the final rubric concerning communion in the prayer book service there is a homily on marriage which is introduced by the words, "After which if there be no sermon, declaring the duties of man and wife, the Minister shall read as followeth."[53] This homily had appeared in all editions of the prayer book since 1549, but Wesley made no provision for a sermon or homily in the matrimonial liturgy in the *Sunday Service*.[54]

Stevenson points out that this monologue originally functioned as a homily at the Eucharist.[55] But just as weekday weddings tended to weaken the connection between matrimony and Eucharist, so they tended to discourage preaching at the wedding service. When weddings take place on Sunday morning, with a full congregation present, a sermon or homily seems in order. But when weddings take place midweek with only a handful of people present, a sermon seems out of place. There is no record of John Wesley preaching a sermon at the wedding of his brother Charles, or at any other wedding. Whether he ever used the wedding homily printed in the prayer book is unknown.

It was not customary for Methodist preachers in either England or America to read published homilies to a congregation. The Large Minutes contain instructions for preachers that make it clear the preachers were expected to prepare their own sermons.

Q. 36. What is the best general method of preaching?
A. (1.) To invite. (2.) To convince. (3.) To offer Christ. (4.) To build up; and to do this in some measure in every sermon.

Q. 37. Are there any smaller advises relative to preaching, which might be of use to us?
A. Perhaps these . . .
(5.) Choose the plainest texts you can.
(6.) Take care not to ramble; but keep to your text, and make out what you take in hand.
(7.) Be sparing in allegorizing or spiritualizing.[56]

These same directions appear in the early American editions of the *Discipline*.[57] In the *Sunday Service*, Wesley deleted all references to the standard Anglican homilies,[58] although Wesley himself thought highly of them.[59] He also removed most long didactic speeches, although the opening address in the service of matrimony was retained.[60]

The reading of a published homily would have been inconsistent with the customs of Methodist preachers, and it is reasonable to conclude that Wesley eliminated the closing homily from the wedding service for that reason. On the other hand, since eighteenth-century weddings were attended by very few people, it would seem odd for a preacher to deliver an original sermon to a congregation of four or five people. Therefore, Wesley eliminated any reference to preaching in the matrimonial rite from the *Sunday Service*.

Music

Neither the Book of Common Prayer nor the *Sunday Service* includes any mention of music in regard to the wedding service. Because music plays such a significant role in wedding services today (and can often be one of the stickiest points of controversy between the bridal couple and the pastor or church musician!), it is appropriate to examine John Wesley's ideas about the use of music in public worship and his practice regarding music in the marriage service.

Organs

Church organs were still objects of controversy in eighteenth-century England.[61] After the dissolution of the monasteries in 1536, there was a growing suspicion of anything connected with the Catholic Church, including organs. The House of Commons listed organ playing as one of the "Faults and Abuses of Religion." In 1563, a resolution in Parliament calling for the removal of all organs from places of worship was defeated by only one vote. In 1644, while the Puritans were in power, Parliament did order the destruction of all church organs, although some survived.[62]

John Wesley was strongly opposed to the use of an organ in Methodist worship. In a letter written just a few months before he died, he explained that he did not object to the presence of an organ in a Methodist chapel, as long as nobody played it![63] The Large Minutes prohibited the installation of an organ in any

Methodist preaching house without the approval of the Conference, the annual gathering of Wesley's preachers.[64] In fact, one recent study of the *Sunday Service* shows that Wesley suppressed all references to instrumental music in his liturgical psalter![65]

However, there are three places in Wesley's journal in which he expresses appreciation for the organ in worship, however grudgingly! The first of these entries is on Easter Day, 1751.

> After preaching, I went to the new church, and found an uncommon blessing, at a time when I least of all expected it; namely, while the Organist was playing a voluntary![66]

In 1762, the organ at Exeter cathedral was able to break down Wesley's defenses and win some words of enthusiastic praise.

> At the cathedral we had an useful sermon, and the whole service was performed with great seriousness and decency. Such an organ I never saw or heard before, so large, beautiful, and so finely toned; and the music of "Glory be to God in the highest," I think exceeded the Messiah itself.[67]

Finally, on Good Friday, 1782, Wesley noted the artistry of a certain organist at Macclesfield.

> I came to Macclesfield just time enough [*sic*] to asist Mr. Simpson in the laborious service of the day. I preached for him morning and afternoon; and we administered the sacrament to about thirteen hundred persons. While we were administering, I heard a low, soft, solemn sound, just like that of an Aeolian harp. It continued five or six minutes, and so affected many, that they could not refrain from tears. It then gradually died away. Strange that no other organist (that I know) should think of this.[68]

But even when describing the skill of this organist, Wesley cannot resist commenting on the limits of such artistry. For immediately after describing the Anglican Good Friday liturgy, Wesley goes on to say, "In the evening, I preached at our [Methodist] Room. Here was that harmony which art cannot imitate."[69]

Choirs

If Wesley disliked organ music in worship, he was no more fond of anthems sung by church choirs. He believed that harmony and counterpoint destroy the power of melody to move the passions.[70] The Large Minutes discouraged the use of complicated melodies and stated flatly, "Sing no anthems."[71] The early American Methodist Disciplines likewise discourage the use of "fuge-tunes," which "puff up with vanity those who excel in them," and raise "an admiration of the singers, and not of Christ."[72]

In the *Sunday Service*, Wesley consistently changed all rubrics which read, "Then shall be said or sung," to "Then shall be said." Service music is expunged from the liturgy, as are all references to anthems.[73]

Wesley's journal yields additional comments regarding his opinion of choral music in worship. On 29 February 1764 Wesley recorded the following observation.

> I heard "Judith," an Oratorio, performed at the Lock. Some parts of it are exceeding fine; but there are two things in all modern pieces of music, which I could never reconcile to common sense. One is singing the same words ten times over; the other, singing different words by different persons, at one and the same time. And this in the most solemn addresses to God, whether by way of prayer or of thanksgiving. This can never be defended by all the musicians in Europe, till reason is quite out of date.[74]

In 1768, Wesley was unexpectedly called upon to preach in a certain church in which he found the manner of singing quite unacceptable.

> When we came to Neath, I was a little surprised to hear I was to preach in the church; of which the Churchwardens had the disposal, the Minister being just dead. I began reading Prayers at six, but was greatly disgusted at the manner of singing. 1. Twelve or fourteen persons kept it to themselves, and quite shut out the congregation: 2. These repeated the same words, contrary to all sense and reason, six or eight or ten times over: 3. According to the shocking custom of modern music, different persons sung different words at one and the same moment; an intolerable insult on common sense, and utterly incompatible with any devotion.[75]

It can hardly be a coincidence that Wesley immediately follows this discussion of Anglican choral music with the entry for the next day: "At five I had the pleasure of hearing the whole congregation at the [Methodist] room 'sing with the spirit and the understanding also'."[76]

In 1781, Wesley discovered to his horror that even in Methodist congregations, people sometimes sang in counterpoint!

The service was at the usual hours. I came just in time to put a stop
to a bad custom, which was creeping in here: A few men, who had
fine voices, sang a Psalm which no one knew, in a tune fit for an
opera, wherein three, four, or five persons, sung different words at
the same time! What an insult upon common sense! What a burlesque
upon public worship! No custom can excuse such a mixture of pro-
faneness and absurdity.[77]

Hymns

The quality of English church music in the eighteenth century
was generally quite poor. Charles Abbey and John Overton, in
their study of the eighteenth-century English church, lay much
of the blame for this state of affairs on the parish clerks. Before
the Reformation, clerks had been a minor order and had served
as assistants to the priests. But by the eighteenth century, "the
Clerk occupied a very odd position, uniting the menial duties of
a useful Church servant to other functions, the decent performance of which was utterly beyond the range of an illiterate man."
One of those functions was the leading of congregational singing.
"No wonder . . . that Church psalmody, under such conditions,
fell into a state which was a reproach to the Church that could
tolerate it."[78]

John Wesley recorded an incident from his youth that is indicative of the depths to which a clerk's performance as song leader
could sometimes sink.

One Sunday, immediately after sermon, my father's clerk said, with
an audible voice, "Let us sing to the praise and glory of God, an hymn
of mine own composing." It was short and sweet, and ran thus:—

King William is come home, come home!
King William home is come!
Therefore let us together sing
The hymn that's call'd Te D'um.[79]

Undoubtedly, it was experiences such as this that Wesley had
in mind when he praised the singing of the Methodists in comparison with the congregational song of the Anglican parishes.

Nor are their solemn addresses to God interrupted either by the
formal drawl of a parish clerk, the screaming of boys, who bawl out
what they neither feel nor understand, or the unseasonable and un-
meaning impertinence of a voluntary on the organ. When it is season-

able to sing praise to God, they do it with the spirit, and with the understanding also; not in the miserable, scandalous doggerel of Hopkins and Sternhold, but in psalms and hymns which are both sense and poetry; such as would sooner provoke a critic to turn Christian, than a Christian to turn critic. What they sing is therefore a proper continuation of the spiritual and reasonable service; being selected for that end (not by a poor humdrum wretch who can scarce read what he drones out with an air of importance, but) by one who knows what he is about, and how to connect the preceding with the following part of the service. Nor does he take just "two staves," but more or less, as may best raise the soul to God; especially when sung in well-composed and well-adapted tunes, not by a handful of wild, unawakened striplings, but by a whole serious congregation; and these, not lolling at ease, or in the indecent posture of sitting, drawling out one word after another, but all standing before God, and praising him lustily and with a good courage.[80]

But if Wesley disliked the singing of the Anglican parishes, the singing of the Dissenters was no better. For when Wesley was speaking to the Methodist Conference of 1755 about how the prayers of a Methodist preacher should differ from those of a Dissenter, he added, "Neither should we sing like them, in a slow drawling manner—we sing swift, both because it saves time and because it tends to awaken and enliven the soul."[81]

We have already noted that a hymn was sung at Charles Wesley's wedding (see page 42), and Charles composed a hymn for the wedding of John and Grace Bennet, although it was sung at dinner rather than in church.[82] We can conclude, therefore, that hymn singing was the only form of music which John Wesley allowed at weddings, just as it was the only form of music he allowed at any other Methodist worship service. But since the number of people present at most weddings was quite small, and some of them were probably not eager hymn singers, it is likely that the singing of a hymn at a wedding during Wesley's lifetime was quite rare.

3

"The Causes for Matrimony"

The Chief Cause

The Anglican View

THE first words spoken in the service of matrimony from the prayer book are an address by the priest which expresses the Anglican understanding of the nature and purpose of marriage. Wesley retained this address without alteration in the *Sunday Service*, although most other didactic exhortations were removed.[1] In it, the priest mentions three "causes for which Matrimony was ordained," namely, procreation, "a remedy against sin," and "the mutual society, help, and comfort, that the one ought to have of the other." These three purposes for marriage were a standard part of western Christian thought since the time of Augustine.[2] And for Anglicans, the first cause mentioned, procreation, was also first in importance. The command to "be fruitful and multiply" from Genesis 1:28 was the principal text defining the institution of marriage.[3]

Articulating the position of the High Churchmen, Richard Hooker wrote:

> In this world there can be no society durable otherwise than only by propagation. Albeit therefore single life be a thing more angelic and divine, yet since the replenishing first of earth with blessed inhabitants and then of heaven with saints praising God did depend upon conjunction of man and woman, he which made all things complete and perfect saw it could not be good to leave man without a helper unto the fore-alleged end. . . .
>
> Now that which is born of man must be nourished with far more travail, as being of greater price in nature and of slower pace to perfection, than the offspring of any other creature besides. Man and woman being therefore to join themselves for such a purpose, they were of necessity to be linked with some strait and insoluble knot.[4]

In this same passage, Hooker speaks of "woman being created for man's sake to be his helper in regard to the end before-mentioned, namely the having and bringing up of children."[5] So for Hooker, even the help and support that husband and wife are to give each other is primarily for the purpose of child rearing and not for the benefit of the marriage partners themselves.

However, the Anglicans were clear that marriage is an "ordinance" of God and not a sacrament; no special grace is given to the couple in the marriage rite. This differed from the Roman Catholic position, which has been summarized as follows.

> In the same way that natural virtues are infused by grace in coopera-tion with human striving to attain these virtues, the grace of matri-mony cooperates with the spouses in their attempts to gain the virtues proper to married life. . . . The sacramental grace present in Christian marriage works through husband and wife to help them realize marriage in all its institutions in their own union.[6]

John Wesley argued against this understanding of marriage in his essay "Popery Calmly Considered."

> The next of their sacraments, so called, is marriage; concerning which they pronounce, "Marriage is truly and properly a sacrament. He that denies it so to be, let him be accursed."
>
> We answer, In one sense it may be so. For St. Austin says, "Signs, when applied to religious things, are called sacraments." In this large sense, he calls the sign of the cross a sacrament; and others give this name to washing the feet. But it is not a sacrament according to the Romish definition of the word; for it no more "confers grace," than washing the feet or signing with the cross.[7]

Wesley speaks of marriage as a divine "ordinance" in his com-ments on Genesis 2:24. "The sabbath and marriage were two ordinances instituted in innocency, the former for the preserva-tion of the church, the latter for the preservation of mankind."[8] Wesley is being completely consistent with the Anglican under-standing of the primary purpose of marriage when he says that it was instituted "for the preservation of mankind."

The Puritan View

Among the Puritans, companionship, and not procreation, was the chief cause for which marriage was ordained. The definitive passage for Puritan marriage doctrine was not Genesis 1:28, but

Genesis 2:18. "The relief of man's loneliness is the primary reason for God's institution of marriage in paradise."[9] The Puritans saw a contradiction in the Anglican doctrine of marriage, for "were the production of children the first end of marriage, polygamy would be preferable as a more efficient means of increasing and multiplying so as to fill the earth."[10] Martin Bucer, in his comments on the matrimonial service in the 1549 edition of the prayer book, articulates the position that would be repeated by later Reformed writers.

> The address which stands at the beginning of this order is excellently godly and holy: nevertheless at about the end of it three causes for matrimony are enumerated, that is children, a remedy, and mutual help, and I should prefer that what is placed third among the causes for marriage might be in the first place, because it is first. For a true marriage can take place between people who seek neither for children nor for a remedy against fornication, as witness not only the marriage of Joseph and Mary but of many others before and after them; and without doubt not a few such are to be encountered today. Yet since "the two are one flesh" and live unto God as one person, it follows that without that union of minds and bodies and possessions by which the husband shows himself to be the head of the wife and the wife a helper of her husband for every purpose of godly and holy living it is no true and real marriage before God.
>
> And so it is that in the first institution of marriage, to which the Lord Christ taught us always to look back, God did not say that its purpose was children, or a remedy, but this: "It is not good for man to be alone, let us therefore make a help for him, to be with him." He says "help" in general terms, by which we may understand that a wife has been given to the man by the Lord, a help not only to avoid fornication and not only to procreate children, but for all the purposes of human life. "For now," says the Lord, "they are not two but one flesh," that is, one person, "and for this reason a man shall leave his father and mother and shall cleave to his wife," meaning, for the work and intercourse of every aspect of life which is lived in gratitude to God.[11]

Notice that, in contrast to Hooker, Bucer emphasizes that woman was created to be a helper in "every aspect of life," not just the bearing and raising of children. In fact, there is evidence that some couples were practicing contraception in seventeenth-century Geneva and eighteenth-century England. While the Genevans tried to prevent pregnancy by coitus interruptus, the English began using condoms. Such a practice was consistent with the Reformed emphasis on marriage as a partnership, rather than as primarily a means of reproduction.[12]

The Puritans believed that God's grace was operative in marriage, but in a way quite different from that taught by the Roman Church.

> In the doctrine of Thomas, grace in marriage operationally *accompanies* and logically *follows* the acts of the partners. . . . When the partners consent to marry, it is their action first, God's action to support them second. . . . For the Puritans, however, grace necessarily *precedes* the decision of two Christian persons to marry and is in a certain way the cause of that decision. . . . In this conception, just as God gave Eve to Adam, so he guides men and women together who will be right for each other.[13]

Divorce and Remarriage

Although Catholics and Anglicans differed as to the sacramental nature of marriage, there was no difference at all in their teachings about divorce.[14] The Anglican Church was the only major ecclesiastical body arising out of the sixteenth-century Reformation that retained, virtually intact, the medieval laws on marriage and divorce.[15] This meant that legal divorce was unobtainable for most people,[16] though a marriage could be annulled on the grounds of a previous marriage contract with somebody else, consanguinity within the prohibited degrees, or male impotence for a period of three years. For couples who no longer wished to live together, a legal separation which included a financial settlement was possible. Although this was popularly called a "divorce," technically the partners were still married to each other, and neither party was permitted to remarry.[17]

By 1670, divorce was permitted, but each divorce required an Act of Parliament, and it was very expensive. By 1750, only seventeen such divorces had been granted. By the end of the eighteenth century, the total had risen to 131.[18]

As we have already noted (see pages 23–24), desertion and bigamy were widespread among those unable to obtain a legal divorce. Sometimes folk rituals evolved as a way of marking the end of an unhappy relationship. One such custom was the so-called "wife sale." In this peculiar ceremony, the husband put a halter around his wife's neck, led her to the marketplace, and auctioned her off to the highest bidder! But lest this sound more like slavery than marriage, it should be noted that generally the whole thing was arranged in advance; both the husband and wife knew beforehand who the "purchaser" would be, and both had agreed to the arrangement.[19]

John Calvin taught that divorce was permissible on the grounds of adultery, and that persons granted a divorce for this reason were free to remarry. His own sister-in-law was divorced for adultery in 1558 and was later permitted to remarry; in 1562 Calvin's stepdaughter was divorced for the same reason. Geneva law permitted either spouse to seek a divorce on the grounds of adultery, desertion, impotence, or frigidity. In practice, men usually sought divorce on the grounds of adultery, women on the grounds of desertion.[20] But petitions for divorce were rarely successful in sixteenth-century Geneva. Following Calvin's example, pastors and the consistory (a group of pastors and elders responsible for overseeing the morality of the city) always pressed couples to find other solutions to their marital problems.[21] Even as late as the beginning of the eighteenth century, Geneva averaged only one divorce a year.[22]

The poet John Milton argued for more lenient divorce laws in seventeenth-century England. Basing his argument on the Puritan teaching that the primary purpose of marriage was not procreation, but the mutual benefit of the marriage partners, Milton believed that no law can force a marriage to continue if the partners were not bound together by mutual affection.[23] He understood the expression "some uncleanness" in the Mosaic divorce law of Deuteronomy 24:1 to signify not just adultery, but "whatever is found to be irreconcilably at variance with love, or fidelity, or help, or society, that is, with the objects of the original institution."[24]

John Wesley, however, supported the idea that divorce is permissible only on the grounds of adultery, and that only persons divorced for this reason are free to marry again. Wesley explains this in his sermon "Upon our Lord's Sermon on the Mount: Discourse III."

> All polygamy is clearly forbidden in these words, wherein our Lord expressly declares, that for any woman who has a husband alive, to marry again is adultery. By parity of reason, it is adultery for any man to marry again, so long as he has a wife alive, yea, although they were divorced; unless that divorce had been for the cause of adultery: In that only case there is no scripture which forbids to marry again.[25]

Wesley regarded the Mosaic divorce laws as a temporary concession to human weakness, and not as a code that could be applied to contemporary Christians. He makes this point in his comments on Deuteronomy 24:1.

> This is not a command as some of the *Jews* understood it, nor an allowance and approbation, but merely a permission of that practice for prevention of greater mischiefs, and this only until *the time of reformation,* till the coming of the *Messiah* when things were to return to their first institution and purest condition.[26]

Wesley discusses this point further in his comments on the teaching of Jesus about divorce in Matthew 19:3–9.

> Christ replies, "Moses permitted," not commanded, "it, because of the hardness of your hearts;" because neither your fathers nor you could bear the more excellent way.
> . . . I revoke that indulgence from this day, so that from henceforth, *Whosoever, &c.*[27]

In the *Sunday Service* Wesley retained the prayer book's citation of the words of Jesus about the indissolubility of marriage in Matthew 19:6 and Mark 10:9, "Those whom God hath joined together, let no man put assunder," as well as the proclamation of marriage which immediately follows. Both of these texts came into the first edition of the Book of Common Prayer from the sixteenth-century German liturgy *A Simple and Religious Consultation* by Hermann von Wied, Archbishop of Cologne.[28] Wesley also retained the closing prayer from the Anglican wedding service which affirms "that it should never be lawful to put asunder those whom thou by Matrimony hadst made one."

The Gift of Continency

The Benefits of Celibacy

But while Anglicans and Puritans debated the chief purpose for marriage, others focused their attention on the second purpose of marriage indicated in the prayer book: "that such persons as have not the gift of Continency, might marry, and keep themselves undefiled members of Christs body."[29] The phrase "have not the gift of continencie" was added to the prayer book in 1552.[30] These were words of special significance for John Wesley, who, even after his own marriage, continued to encourage his followers to remain single if at all possible.

In the diary that records Wesley's romance with Grace Murray, there is a section in which he traces how his personal feelings about marriage developed over the years. As this excerpt from his diary shows, his positive regard for celibacy went back to his early childhood!

1. From the time I was Six or Seven years old, if any one spoke to me concerning marrying, I used to say, I thought I never should, "Because I should never find such a Woman as my Father had."

2. When I was about Seventeen (and so till I was Six or Seven and twenty) I had no thought of marrying, "Because I could not keep a Wife."

3. I was then persuaded, "It was unlawful for a Priest to marry," grounding that Persuasion on the (supposed) Sense of the Primitive Church.

4. Not long after, by reading some of the Mystic Writers, I was brought to think "Marriage was the less Perfect state," and that there was some degree (at least) of "Taint upon the Mind, necessarily attending the Marriage-Bed."

5. At the same time I view'd in a strong light St. Paul's words to the Corinthians: And judg'd it "impossible for a married man to be so without carefulness, or to attend upon the Lord with so little Distraction, as a single man might do."

6. Likewise, being desirous to lay out all I could in feeding the hungry and cloating [sic] the naked, I could not think of marrying, "because it would bring such Expense, as would swallow up all I now give away."

7. But my grand Objection for these twelve years past has been, "A Dispensation of the Gospel has been committed to me. And I will do nothing which directly or indirectly tends to hinder my preaching the Gospel."[31]

In 1743, Wesley published his *Thoughts on Marriage and a Single Life*, in which he argued that *every* believer is given the gift of continence at the time of his or her conversion!

All Men (as our Lord had observ'd before) *cannot receive this Saying: But they*, and they only, *to whom it is given*, by the Giver of every Good and Perfect Gift: . . .

Hence it plainly appears, That *they who were able to receive this Saying*, are they *to whom* Continence *is given;* they who having *this Gift of* GOD, can *avoid Fornication*, . . .

"But who are able to keep themselves thus pure?" I answer, Every Believer in CHRIST: Every one who hath living Faith *in the Name of the only begotten Son of* GOD. . . . Whoever find *Redemption in his Blood*, in that Hour receives this Gift of GOD. Lust then vanishes away: And if they that are *born of* GOD, *keep* themselves, shall never return.[32]

Wesley was careful to distinguish his teaching from that of Roman Catholic writers who regarded celibacy not as a command for all Christians, but as a "counsel of the Gospel" for the spiritual elite.

> Indeed the *Romish* Writers in general affirm of This, "That it is a *Counsel* not a *Command*." But their whole Doctrine of "Evangelical Counsels, contradistinguished from Divine Commands," is plainly designed to make Way for a still worse Doctrine, That of Works of Supererogation, "It is our *Duty* (say they) to keep the *Commands* of GOD; To keep the *Counsels* is *Supererogation*." But we allow of no such Distinction as this; because we find it not in Holy Writ. It has no Place in Scripture. And least of all, here. For the Word is Peremptory. *Choreito. Let him receive it.* (Not, He *may* receive it, if he *will*.) How could a Command be more clearly exprest?[33]

Anyone who married was therefore throwing away the gift of God that had been given with regeneration. Some of Wesley's preachers objected to this idea, and at the Methodist Conference of 1748, they discussed their objections with Wesley.

> In June 1748 we had a Conference in London. Several of our Brethren then objected to the Thoughts upon Marriage, and in a full and friendly debate convinced me That a Believer might marry, without suffering Loss in his Soul.[34]

In 1764, Wesley wrote his "Thoughts on a Single Life," in which he contradicted his 1743 essay *Thoughts on Marriage and a Single Life* and acknowledged that not everyone is able to remain celibate.

> But though "it is good for a man not to touch a woman," (verse 1,) yet this is not an universal rule. "I would," indeed, says the Apostle, "that all men were as myself." (verse 7.) But that cannot be; for "every man hath his proper gift of God, one after this manner, another after that."[35]

But even at this point in his life, having been married for thirteen years, Wesley still maintained that every believer is given the gift of continency concurrently with justification, and that the loss of that gift probably indicates some fault on the part of the believer!

> But who is able to "receive this saying"—to abstain from marriage, and yet not burn? It behoves [*sic*] every one here to judge for himself:

none is called to judge for another. In general, I believe every man is able to receive it when he is first justified. I believe every one then receives this gift; but with most it does not continue long. This much is clear; it is a plain matter of fact, which no man can deny. It is not so clear, whether God withdraws it of his own good pleasure, or for any fault of ours. I incline to think it is not withdrawn without some fault on our part.[36]

Wesley warned unmarried people that if they did not make use of the advantages of continency, they were in danger of losing their gift.

I advise you, Lastly, if you desire to keep them, use all the advantages you enjoy. Indeed, without this, it is utterly impossible to keep them; for the mouth of the Lord hath spoken the word which cannot be broken, which must be fulfilled with regard to all the good gifts of God: "To him that hath," uses what he hath, "shall be given; and he shall have more abundantly: But from him that hath not," uses it not, "shall be taken even that which he hath."[37]

Wesley consistently emphasizes what a great blessing it is to be given this gift. In his comments on Matthew 19:12, he speaks of the happy state of those who have received such a blessing.

Happy they, who have abstained from marriage (though without condemning or despising it) that they might walk more closely with God! . . . This gracious command . . . is not designed for all men; but only those few who are "able to receive it." O let those receive it joyfully![38]

In his comments on 1 Corinthians 7:7, Wesley speaks again of "the happy few" who were able to remain unmarried.[39]

Wesley consistently urged his followers to remain single whenever possible. Four days after deciding that he himself would marry, Wesley made the following entry in his journal.

I met the single men, and showed them on how many accounts it was good for those who had received that gift from God to remain "single for the kingdom of heaven's sake"; unless where a particular case might be an exception to the general rule.[40]

In the last decade of his life, Wesley was still encouraging celibacy, as we can see from a letter he wrote in 1781.

I commend you for being exceeding wary with respect to marriage. St. Paul's direction is full and clear: "If thou mayest be free, use it rather." "Art thou loosed from a wife? Seek not a wife." Two of our small tracts you should read with much prayer—*Thoughts on a Single Life* and *A Word to Whom it may Concern.*[41]

One of the writers who most strongly influenced John Wesley's thinking was the seventeenth-century Anglican bishop Jeremy Taylor.[42] In his classic devotional work, *The Rules and Exercise of Holy Living,* Taylor had written of the advantages of the celibate life.

Virginity is a life of angels, the enamel of the soul, the huge advantage of religion, the great opportunity for the retirements of devotion. And being empty of cares it is full of prayers; being unmingled with the world, it is apt to converse with God; and by not feeling the warmth of nature, flames out with holy fires, till it be burning like the cherubim and the most ecstasied order of high and unpolluted spirits.

Virginity of itself is not a state more acceptable to God; but that which is chosen in order to [sic] the conveniences of religion, and is therefore better than the married life, not that it is more holy, but that it is a freedom from cares, an opportunity to spend more time in spiritual employments; it is not allayed with business and attendances upon lower affairs.[43]

Taylor's influence can be observed in Wesley's "Thoughts on a Single Life." Wesley there argues that singles can "attend upon the Lord without distraction." They are exempt from "domestic trials" and can devote all their time, talents, and "worldly substance" to God.[44] Most importantly, single persons are better able to love God wholeheartedly because their loyalty is not divided between God and a spouse.

Above all, you are at liberty from the greatest of all entanglements, the loving one creature above all others. It is possible to do this without sin, without any impeachment of our love to God. But how inconceivably difficult! to give God our whole heart, while a creature has so large a share of it! How much more easily may we do this, when the heart is, tenderly indeed, but equally attached to more than one; or, at least, without any great inequality! What angelic wisdom does it require to give enough of our affection, and not too much, to so near a relation!

And how much easier it is (just to touch on one point more) wholly to conquer our natural desires, than to gratify them exactly so far as Christian temperance allows! just so far as every pleasure of sense prepares us for taking pleasure in God.[45]

Wesley's constant emphasis was that no rival must be allowed to dethrone God from the preeminent place in a believer's life. Wesley made this point in "A Thought upon Marriage" published in 1785.

> Were you ever convinced of sin? . . . If so, what did you then want to make you happy? . . .
> . . . If, therefore, you are not happy now, is it not because you have not that intercourse with God which you then had? And are you seeking to supply the want of that intercourse by the enjoyment of a creature? You imagine that near connexion [sic] with a woman will make amends for distance from God![46]

Reflecting on his response when he discovered that his brother had ridden off with Grace Murray, presumably to take her to John Bennet, Wesley wrote in his diary,

> If I had had more Regard for her I loved, than for the Work of God, I should have gone strait [sic] to Newcastle, and not back to Whitehaven. I knew this was giving up all: But I knew God call'd: And therefore, on Friday 29, set out.[47]

In 1777 Wesley urged a Methodist widower not to marry again.[48] And in 1770 he urged a prospective bride to consider how marriage would affect her usefulness to God.

> If, indeed, you could enlarge the sphere of your action; if you could be more extensively useful; or if you could have a closer union than you ever had yet with a person of very eminent grace and understanding, I should instantly acknowledge the call of God and say, "Go, and the Lord will be with thee!" But I can see nothing of this in your present case.[49]

Perhaps nowhere is Wesley's position summarized more succinctly than in the verse he wrote in 1746 as a forty-three-year-old bachelor. Although Wesley eventually married, he never wandered far from the attitude expressed here.

> I have no sharer of my heart
> To rob my Saviour of a part
> And desecrate the whole;
> Only betrothed to Christ am I
> And wait his coming from the sky
> To wed my happy soul.[50]

Avoiding Sexual Temptation

Wesley acknowledged that persons who decide to remain single have chosen a difficult course for themselves. The temptation to cast aside the gift of God is ever present.

> Not only the children of the world, but the children of God will undoubtedly tempt you thereto; and that partly by the most plausible reasons, partly by the most artful persuasions. Meanwhile, the old deceiver will not be wanting to give an edge to all those reasons and persuasions, and to recall the temptation again and again, and press it close upon your heart.[51]

In his 1764 "Thoughts on a Single Life," Wesley offers four suggestions for the person who earnestly seeks to avoid marriage. The first of these recommendations is frequent, earnest prayer. Wesley advised his followers to "let no day pass" without asking God "to preserve his own gift" and protect it from "the subtlety or power of devils or men, or the deceitfulness of your own heart."[52]

Wesley's second recommendation was the support of like-minded friends of the same sex.

> It may be of infinite service to disclose to these the very secrets of your hearts; especially the weaknesses springing from your natural constitution, or education, or long-contracted habit, and the temptations which, from time to time, most easily beset you. Advise them on every circumstance that occurs; open your heart without reserve. By this means a thousand devices of Satan will be brought to nought; innumerable snares will be prevented; or you will pass through them without being hurt. Yea, and if at some time you should have suffered a little, the wound will speedily be healed.[53]

But if supportive companions of the same sex are of great help in avoiding temptation, companionship with the opposite sex is a deadly snare that is to be avoided whenever possible. This was Wesley's third recommendation.

> . . . it will be highly expedient to avoid all needless conversation, much more all intimacy, with those of the other sex; so expedient, that unless you observe this, you will surely cast away the gift of God. Say not, "But they have much grace and much understanding." So much the greater is the danger. There would be less fear of your receiving hurt from them, if they had less grace or less understanding. And whenever any of these are thrown in your way, "make a covenant with your eyes," your ears, your hands, that you do not

indulge yourself in any that are called innocent freedoms. Above all, "keep your heart with all diligence." Check the first risings of desire. Watch against every sally of imagination, particularly if it be pleasing.[54]

Wesley warns against the dangers of dancing when he quotes with approval the words of an Anglican bishop, "The ambushes of evil spirits carry away many souls from dancing to a fearful desolation."[55]

Masturbation, of course, was never acceptable as a way of releasing sexual tension. Like others of his era, Wesley believed that thousands of persons had become seriously ill and even died because of habitual masturbation. In *Thoughts on the Sin of Onan*, Wesley documents many such cases and even recommends specific methods of treatment for each of these maladies.[56]

Wesley's fourth recommendation to those desiring to avoid sexual temptation was the practice of asceticism.

> Avoid all delicacy, first in spirit, then in apparel, food, lodging, and a thousand nameless things, and this the more speedily and the more resolutely, if you have been long accustomed thereto. Avoid all needless self-indulgence, as well as delicacy and softness. All these tend to breed or cherish those appetites and passions which you have renounced for Christ's sake. They either create or increase those desires which, "For the kingdom of heaven's sake," you are determined not to gratify. Avoid all sloth, inactivity, indolence. Sleep no more than nature requires. Be never idle; and use as much bodily exercise as your strength will allow. . . . Add to your other exercises constant and prudent fasting, and the Lord will uphold you with his hand.[57]

Wesley summarized this point elsewhere when he wrote, "The bed of sloth often proves the bed of lust."[58]

The Benefits of Marriage

But despite Wesley's strong support of celibacy, he came to recognize that it was better for some people to marry. Richard Hooker had already acknowledged that although a life of virginity was "more angelic and divine," the survival of the human race depended upon procreation (see pages 52–53). Jeremy Taylor recognized that

> . . . some married persons even in their marriage do better please God than some virgins in their state of virginity. They, by giving great

example of conjugal affection, by preserving their faith unbroken, by educating children in the fear of God, by patience and contentedness and holy thoughts and the exercise of virtues proper to that state, do not only please God, but do it in a higher degree than those virgins whose piety is not answerable to their great opportunities and advantages.[59]

Wesley read the testimony of some who reported not only that marriage was no hindrance to their service of God, but that marriage actually helped them to serve God better. A Puritan minister named James Fraser described how, after moving into a new home with his wife, he had opportunities to preach much more frequently and to many more people than he ever had in the place where he had lived as a bachelor.[60] Even in the 1743 *Thoughts on Marriage and a Single Life,* in which Wesley argued that every believer was able to remain celibate, he also made the rather contradictory statement that marriage was not to be forbidden or despised.[61] And in "The Character of a Methodist," he noted that it was not characteristic of Methodists to abstain from marriage.[62]

By 1748 Wesley came to recognize that the reasons he had listed for not marrying previously (see page 58) had all been removed.

My first Objection was easily removed by my finding some, though very few Women, whom I could not but allow to be equal to my Mother, both in Knowledge and Piety.

My Second, "that I could not keep a Wife," held only till I found reason to believe, there were persons in the world, who if I were so inclined, were both able and wiling to keep *me.*

My Third vanished away when I read with my own Eyes Bishop Beverege's *Codex Conciliorum.* I then found the very Council of Nice had determined just the contrary to what I had supposed [regarding the marriage of clergy].

St. Paul slowly and gradually awakened me out of my Mystic Dream; and convinced me, "The bed is undefiled, and no necessary Hindrance to the Highest Perfection." Though still I did not quite shake off the weight, till our last Conference in London.

I was next, though very unwillingly convinced, That there might be such a Case as Dr. Koker's: who often declared, He was never so free from Care, never served God with so little distraction, as since his Marriage with one, who was both able and willing to bear that Care for him.

The two other Objections weighed with me still, Increase of Expence and Hindering the Gospel. But with regard to the former, I now clearly perceive, That my Marriage would bring little Expence, if I married one I maintain now [i.e., Grace Murray, his household servant], who would afterward desire nothing more than she had before: And would chearfully [sic] consent, That our Children (if any) should be wholly brought up at Kingswood.

As to the latter, I have the strongest Assurance, which the nature of the Thing will allow, that the person proposed would not hinder, but exceedingly further me in the Work of the Gospel. For, from a close Observation of several Years (three of which she spent under my own roof) I am persuaded she is in every Capacity an Help meet for me.[63]

Wesley recorded in his diary that it was his love for Grace Murray that finally cured him of "unholy desires."

She is and would be a continual Defence (under GOD) against unholy Desires and inordinate Affections: Which I never did entirely conquer, for six months together, before my intercourse with her.[64]

When Wesley decided to marry Molly Vazeille in 1751, he wrote in his journal,

For many years I remained single, because I believed I could be more useful in a single than in a married state. And I praise God who enabled me so to do. I now as fully believed that in my present circumstances I might be more useful in a married state.[65]

In 1763 he wrote in a letter, "Certainly it is possible for persons to be as devoted to God in a married as in a single state."[66] Twenty years later, Wesley told a new bride that she could continue to serve God as a married woman, just as his mother had done.

In the new sphere of action to which Providence has called you, I trust you will find new zeal for God and new vigour in pursuing every measure which may tend to the furtherance of His kingdom. In one of my mother's letters you may observe something resembling your case. She began only with permitting two or three of her neighbors to come to the family prayers on Sunday evening. But they increased to an hundred, yea above an hundred and fifty.[67]

And in 1789 Wesley acknowledged to another of his female followers that, despite his fears, marriage had not harmed either her spirituality or her discipleship.

When I first heard of your marriage, I was afraid of two things: The one was, that it would hurt your soul; the other, that it would prevent your usefulness; at least, that you would not be useful in so high a degree as otherwise you might be. But your last letter has given me much satisfaction. I now hope that your own soul has suffered no loss; and likewise, that you will find many opportunities of doing good, and will improve them to the uttermost.[68]

Sex in Marriage

Wesley urged persons to remain single if possible because he believed that the single life, as a general rule, permitted greater service to God than did a married life. But he did not teach that sexual abstinence was virtuous in and of itself. Wesley makes this point right at the beginning of his 1764 "Thoughts on a Single Life."

> The forbidding to marry, as it is well known the Church of Rome does, and has done for several ages, (in which marriage is absolutely forbidden, not only to all religious orders, but to the whole body of the Clergy,) is numbered, by the great Apostle, among "the doctrines of devils." And among the same we need not scruple to number the despising or condemning marriage; as do many of those in the Romish Church who are usually termed Mystic writers. One of these does not scruple to affirm, "Marriage is only licensed fornication." But the Holy Ghost says, "Marriage is honourable in all, and the bed undefiled." Nor can it be doubted but persons may be as holy in a married as in a single state.
>
> In that latter clause of the sentence, the Apostle seems to guard against a mistake, into which some sincere Christians have fallen; particularly when they have just found such a liberty of spirit as they had not before experienced. They imagine a defilement where there is none, "and fear where no fear is." And it is possible this very fear of sin may betray them into sin. For it may induce persons to defraud each other, forgetting the express determination of the Apostle: "The wife hath not power of her own body, but the husband; and the husband hath not power of his own body, but the wife."[69]

Commenting on 1 Corinthians 7:3–4 in his *Explanatory Notes upon the New Testament*, Wesley cautions, "Let not married persons fancy that there is any perfection in living with each other, as if they were unmarried. . . . Let no one forget this, on pretence of greater purity."[70] Even though Leviticus 12:2 teaches that a woman who gives birth to a son is unclean for seven days following the birth, Wesley says that this teaching was given "not for any filthiness which was either in the conception, or in bringing forth, but to signify the universal and deep pollution of man's nature, even from the birth, and from the conception."[71]

The prayer book said that one of the purposes of marriage was "to avoid fornication," and Wesley heartily concurred with that opinion. In his comments on 1 Corinthians 7:5, Wesley says that married couples may agree to abstain from sex temporarily so they may devote themselves to "exercises of devotion," but he cautions that they not continue in that state for long, lest they be tempted "to unclean thoughts, if not actions too."[72]

But Wesley taught that even within marriage there can be such a thing as sexual excess. Marriage does not mean "anything goes"; there are limits even within matrimony. Wesley wrote, "Content thyself with those delights which God alloweth thee in the sober use of the marriage-bed." Commenting on Proverbs 5:19, Wesley says that this verse refers to sexual enjoyment "at all convenient times: for that there may be excess in the marriage-bed is manifest."[73]

The Marriage of Clergy

English clergy were first permitted to marry legally under the reign of Edward VI,[74] but popular acceptance of married clergy came slowly. At the end of a visit to the residence of Archbishop of Canterbury Matthew Parker, Queen Elizabeth I thanked the archbishop's wife for her hospitality in these strange words: "And you—madam I may not call you, mistress I am ashamed to call you, so I know not what to call you—but, howsoever, I thank you."[75] Even as late as Wesley's lifetime, a noblewoman complained that girls from good families were marrying curates and, even worse, the Earl of Huntingdon's daughter had "disposed of herself to a poor wandering Methodist."[76]

As a young man, John Wesley believed that the early church had forbidden the marriage of clergy (see page 58), and since he tried to follow the practice of the early church as closely as possible, he resolved never to marry. But when he discovered that he had been mistaken about ancient Christian practice, he reversed his position and argued that clergy had as much right to marry as did anyone else. Wesley states his viewpoint succinctly in "Popery Calmly Considered."

> A more dangerous error in the Church of Rome is, the forbidding the Clergy to marry. "Those that are married may not be admitted into orders: Those that are admitted may not marry: And those that, being admitted, do marry, are to be separated."
>
> The Apostle, on the contrary, says, "Marriage is honourable in all;"

(Heb. xiii. 4;) and accuses those who "forbid to marry," of teaching "doctrines of devils." How lawful it was for the Clergy to marry, his directions concerning it show. (1 Tim. iv. 1, 3.) And how convenient, yea, necessary, in many cases it is, clearly appears from the innumerable mischiefs which have in all ages followed the prohibition of it in the Church of Rome; which so many wise and good men, even of her own communion, have lamented.[77]

Commenting on Hebrews 13:4 in his *Explanatory Notes Upon the New Testament*, Wesley had this to say:

Marriage is honourable in, or for *all* sorts of *men*, clergy as well as laity; though the Romanists teach otherwise. *And the bed undefiled*— Consistent with the highest purity; though many spiritual writers, so called, say it is only licensed whoredom.[78]

When Titus 1:6 says that an elder must be "the husband of one wife," Wesley editorializes, "Surely the Holy Ghost, by repeating this so often, designed to leave the Romanists without excuse."[79] Wesley gets in another jab at the papists when he shows that the teachings of the Roman Church regarding marriage and abstinence match the New Testament's description of those who "depart from the faith, giving heed to seducing spirits, and doctrines of devils." They do this by "*forbidding* priests, monks, and nuns *to marry, and commanding* all men *to abstain from* such and such *meats* at such and such times."[80] Wesley also noted that prophets, priests, and Levites, "though they were wholly devoted to sacred employments, were not excluded from marriage."[81]

But even though he faulted the Roman Church for not allowing priests to marry, Wesley himself strongly encouraged his Methodist preachers to remain single, because he feared a married preacher would not be able to serve as freely as would a single man. (It should be noted that most of the early Methodist preachers were lay preachers, not ordained clergy.)

Wesley saw evidence of how marriage can cripple a preacher's effectiveness in the case of Westley Hall. Westley Hall, who had recently married John Wesley's sister, was to accompany John and Charles to Georgia in 1735. The Bishop of London had ordained him both deacon and priest and had appointed him minister of Savannah. The day before departure, he told the founder of the colony "his wife was unwilling to go to Georgia, and all his relations unwilling he should go; that his uncle had promised to procure him a living, and so he resolved to stay in England!"[82]

In 1767, Wesley advised one of his preachers who was contemplating marriage to be very clear with his fiancée about what marriage to a Methodist preacher would entail.

> I advise you to tell her immediately, either in person or by letter (whichever you think safest), "I dare not settle in any one place: God has called me to be a travelling preacher. Are you willing to accept of me upon these terms? And can you engage never directly or indirectly to hinder me from travelling? If not, it is best for us to part. It cannot be avoided."[83]

In 1782 Wesley wrote to a preacher named Zachariah Yewdall and advised him to remain single.

> Read the *Thoughts upon a Single Life,* and weigh them well. You will then feel the wisdom of St. Paul's advice (especially to a preacher, and to a Methodist preacher above all), "If thou mayest be free, use it rather."[84]

In 1789 Wesley wrote to one of his preachers to congratulate him on escaping from a close brush with matrimony.

> You send me good news indeed. I congratulate you upon your deliverance. It is not a little one. Only He that is almighty was able to burst those bonds in sunder. Many years ago I was in exactly the same case; and just then, when I came to these words in the Lesson for the day, "Son of man, behold I take from thee the desire of thine eyes with a stroke," I was quite stunned, and could not just then read a word more. But afterwards I saw God was wiser than me.
> · It seems to me that you drew the right conclusion from this remarkable providence. Surely God does now give you a loud call to devote yourself to God in a single life. I advise you to read with much prayer the *Notes* on I Corinthians 7th. And remember the wise direction of Kempis, "Avoid all *good women,* and commend them to God."[85]

In addition to Wesley's prodding, there were also formal policies to discourage the marriage of preachers. Methodist preachers were required to "take no step toward Marriage, without first consulting your brethren." A preacher who married during his initial probationary period was thereby disqualified.[86] Wesley wrote, "I dare not exclude those who marry out of our Connexion, or forbid to marry; but happy are those who, having no necessity laid upon them, stand fast in the glorious liberty."[87]

The marriage of Methodist preachers eventually caused financial difficulties for the Methodist Conference. In 1790, Wesley wrote in a letter:

I say to you as to every other Preacher, "If thou mayest be free, use it rather." But I have no right to use a constraint, only I must remind you, that if I live to another Conference, I must inform all our Brethren that we cannot provide for any more Preachers wives: so that whatever Preachers marry for the time to come; must themselves provide for them.[88]

And although he was persuaded in 1748 that "a Believer might marry, without suffering Loss in his Soul,"[89] his persistent emphasis on the value of the single life understandably gave some of his preachers the impression that he regarded marriage as a sin. We see evidence of this in a letter written from Glasgow by one of those preachers in 1785.

It is an unkah [sic] thing indeed that Mr. W. should still endeavour to make us believe that marriage is sinful in the light of God, when at the same time an apostle tells us it is honourable in all men. For my own part, I dinna ken what interpretation he puts upon such Scriptures. But from hence you will see that we cannot with safety call any man Rabbi.[90]

In his own case, Wesley was careful that marriage did not interfere with his work as a preacher. Before marrying Molly Vazeille, he insisted to her that their marriage must not prevent him from traveling or preaching any less than he was accustomed to do. "If I thought it would be otherwise," he told her, "much as I love you, I would see your face no more."[91] A month after his wedding, Wesley congratulated himself in his journal on not allowing marriage to interfere with his ministry.

I cannot understand how a Methodist preacher can answer it to God to preach one sermon or travel one day less in a married than in a single state. In this respect surely "it remaineth that they who have wives be as though they had none."[92]

Wesley's marriage was not a happy one, as we shall see in chapter 5, and in later life, he told his assistant Henry Moore that the hand of God had been at work, even in his unhappy marriage. For "if Mrs. Wesley had been a better wife, he might have been unfaithful to the great work to which God had called him, and might have too much sought to please her according to her own views."[93] A similar opinion had been expressed in 1776 by a preacher named John Berridge, who had been tempted by a "Jezebel" himself, but had been rescued by "divine intelligence." Observing the effect that marriage had upon John and Charles Wesley and upon George Whitefield, Berridge commented, "No trap so mischievous to the field preacher as wedlock. . . . Matrimony has quite maimed poor Charles, and might have spoiled John and George, if a wise Master had not graciously sent them a pair of ferrets."[94]

Surely the Lord works in mysterious ways!

A Case History: John Wesley and Sophia Hopkey

Wesley's determination to remain single was put to its most severe test when he was thirty-two years old and serving as a missionary pastor in Georgia.[95] Wesley wrote in his diary, "At my first coming to Savannah, in the beginning of March 1736, I was determined to have no intimacy with any woman in America." But by 22 March Wesley was already feeling his resolve being tested. He wrote to his brother Charles, "I stand in jeopardy every hour. Two or three [of the colonists] are women, younger, refined, God-fearing. Pray that I know none of them after the flesh."[96] The chief cause of Wesley's discomfort was Miss Sophia Hopkey, the seventeen-year-old niece of the chief magistrate of the colony, Thomas Causton. She was one of his most regular worship attenders, and, in contrast to the casual attitude toward religion exemplified by most of the colonists, he was impressed with how "very serious" she was.

In early July, Mrs. Causton asked Wesley to speak privately to her niece. "Miss Sophy" (as Wesley always called her) was resolved to marry a man named Thomas Mellichamp who was in prison in Charleston for forgery. Wesley spoke with Sophy for about an hour, "at the end of which she said she was resolved to seek comfort in God only, and through his help to tear from her heart an inclination which she knew did not tend to his glory."

Over the next few weeks, Wesley saw Sophy more frequently. He recorded that on one of those occasions, "after I had talked with her for some time, I took her by the hand and, before we parted, kissed her." Sophy's aunt and uncle were delighted with the relationship that was developing between their niece and the new pastor. Mrs. Causton had already told Wesley that he needed a woman to take care of his house. When Wesley objected that women were scarce in Georgia, she suggested Sophy to him. Wesley exclaimed, "You are not in earnest, madam!" She responded, "Indeed, sir, I am; take her to you, and do what you will with her."

In October Wesley had an equally frank discussion with Sophy's uncle. Mr. Causton said of his niece, "The girl will never be easy till she is married." Wesley commented, "But there are few here whom you would think fit for her." Causton said that all he wanted for Sophy was a good, honest man. It did not matter if Sophy's husband had no money because Causton would be able to maintain them financially. Wesley then asked, "Sir, what directions do you give me with regard to her?" Causton replied, "I give her up to you. Do what you will with her. Take her into your own hands. Promise her what you will; I will make it good."

In the autumn of 1736 Sophy spent several weeks in Frederica, a small settlement on St. Simons Island about a hundred miles south of Savannah. Wesley, who had also been in Frederica for a short time, accompanied her on the return trip to Savannah. Wesley was aware of the risks involved in traveling together, but he believed that they were both determined to remain single, and he was counting on that determination to save them from any impropriety.

They set sail on Monday, 25 October. In the evening they landed on an uninhabited island where they camped for the night. Wesley recorded in his diary that even though they slept next to each other all night, there was no sexual contact between them.

> I can never be sensible enough of the exceeding goodness of God, both this night and the four following, all of which we spent together, while none but the All-seeing Eye observed us. To him alone be the praise that we were both withheld from anything which the world counts evil.

Wesley does, however, admit that at one o'clock that morning, lying next to Sophy, he was guilty of "sins of thought." On Friday evening, as they lay side by side on the ground, Wesley and Sophy talked of marriage.

> Observing in the night, the fire we lay by burning bright, that Miss Sophy was broad awake, I asked her, "Miss Sophy, how far are you engaged to Mr. Mellichamp?" She answered, "I have promised either to marry him or to marry no one at all." I said (which indeed was the expression of a sudden wish, not of any forward design), "Miss Sophy, I should think myself happy if I was to spend my life with you." She burst out into tears and said, "I am every way unhappy. I won't have Tommy for he is a bad man. And I can have none else."

The next afternoon, Sophy told Wesley that she could not bear to live with the Caustons any longer. When they landed in Savannah, Wesley spoke with Mr. Causton and suggested that Sophy should spend every morning and a part of the evening at Wesley's house studying French, reading devotional literature, singing psalms, and praying with him. This meant that Sophy need stay at the Caustons' home only at night and in the afternoon. Causton readily agreed to this proposal.

But Wesley soon found that such frequent contact with Sophy was posing a serious challenge to his commitment to celibacy.

> My desire and design still was to live single. But how long it would continue I knew not. . . .
> . . . My greatest difficulty was while I was teaching her French, when being obliged (as having but one book) to sit close to her, unless I prayed without ceasing I could not avoid using some familiarity or other which was not needful. Sometimes I put my arm round her waist, sometimes took her by the hand, and sometimes kissed her.

On 10 November Wesley told Sophy that he did not like the way he was acting toward her and resolved never to touch her again. He noted that "she appeared surprised and deeply serious, but said not one word." But Wesley soon discovered that keeping such a commitment was no easy matter.

> For ten days I kept firm to my resolution; but on November 20, as we sat together, I took her by the hand (though I was convinced it was wrong), and kissed her once or twice. I resolved again and relapsed again several times during the five or six weeks following.

In January, while Wesley was visiting in Frederica, a group of friends there told him how happy they would be if he were to marry Sophia Hopkey. Wesley responded, "Why do you talk so idly? You know she is resolved 'not to marry at all'?" But a woman named Phoebe Hird said that Sophy had told her she would never marry anyone but Tom Mellichamp, "unless it was a very religious man. But when I asked her, what if Mr. Wesley would have her, she smiled, looked down, and said nothing." Wesley then perceived that it was purely his own resistance, and not Sophy's, that stood between him and matrimony.

> I was now in a great strait. I still thought it best for me to live single, and this was still my design, but I felt the foundations of it shaken more and more every day. Insomuch that on Thursday, February 3, I again used the familiarities I had resolved against. And likewise again hinted at a desire of marriage, though I made no direct proposal. For

indeed it was only a sudden thought, which had not the consent of my own mind. Yet I firmly believe, had she closed with me at that time, my judgment would have made but a faint resistance. But she said, she thought it was best for clergymen not be encumbered with worldly cares; and that it was best for her too to live single, and she was accordingly resolved "never to marry." I used no argument to induce her to alter her resolution.

Two days later, Wesley asked one of the Moravian pastors in Savannah if he should end his relationship with Sophia Hopkey. The pastor asked him, "And what do you think would be the consequence if you should not break it off?" Wesley replied, "I fear I should marry her." The pastor answered, "I don't see why you should not." Wesley was utterly amazed at this response. He wrote in his diary, "It was now first that I had the least doubt whether it was best for me to marry or not. Which I never before thought would bear a question."

Wesley's associate Benjamin Ingham recommended that Wesley leave town for a few days to think things over. Wesley took Ingham's advice, but before leaving, he wrote a letter to Sophy, explaining his departure.

> I find, Miss Sophy, I can't take fire into my bosom, and not be burned. I am therefore retiring for a while, to desire the direction of God. Join with me, my friend, in fervent prayer, that he would show me what is best to be done.

When Wesley returned to Savannah several days later, his resolve to remain single was strengthened. On 14 February (an ironic date for such an announcement), Wesley told Sophy that he was determined not to marry because he feared it would obstruct his intention of doing missionary work among the Indians. In response to Wesley's announcement, Sophy told him the next morning that she would no longer eat breakfast at his house, nor would she come to his home alone any more. And the following day, she discontinued her French lessons. "But," she added, "My uncle and aunt, as well as I, will be glad of your coming to our house as often as you please." Wesley objected, "You know, Miss Sophy, I don't love a crowd, and there is always one there." She replied coyly, "But we needn't be in it. We may be in the garden, or under the shed, or anywhere."

But in spite of the decrease in the hours he spent with Sophy, Wesley still found their time together to be an overwhelming challenge to his commitment to celibacy, as we can see from his diary entry for 26 February 1737.

> Calling at Mr. Causton's, she was there alone. And this was indeed an hour of trial. Her words, her eyes, her air, her every motion and gesture, were full of such a softness and sweetness! I know not what might have been the consequences had I then but touched her hand. And how I avoided it I know not. Surely God is over all!

Wesley recorded a similar encounter the very next day.

> After all the company but Miss Sophy was gone, Mr. Delamotte went out and left us alone again. Finding her still the same, my resolution failed. At the end of a very serious conversation, I took her by the hand and kissed her twice; and perceiving she was not dis[pleased], I was so utterly disarmed that this hour I should have engaged myself for life had it not been for the full persuasion I had of her entire sincerity; in consequence of which I doubted not but she was resolved (as she had said) "never to marry while she lived."

On Friday, 4 March, after a long and serious discussion about Miss Sophy, Wesley and his associate Charles Delamotte "agreed to appeal to the Searcher of Hearts." Wesley prepared three lots, of which one said, "Marry," one said, "Think not of it this year," and one said, "Think of it no more." After praying to God for "a perfect lot," Delamotte drew the lot that said, "Think of it no more." A second lot was cast to determine whether or not Wesley should continue to converse with her. The answer was "only in the presence of Mr. Delamotte."

On Tuesday, 8 March Sophy had breakfast with Wesley and Delamotte. Wesley asked her, "I hear Mr. Williamson pays his addresses to you. Is it true?" (William Williamson was Mr. Causton's clerk who was living at the Caustons' home.) Sophy replied, after some hesitation, "If it were not I would have told you so." Wesley asked, "How do you like him?" She answered, "I don't know; there is a great deal in being always in the house with one. But I have no inclination for him." Wesley told her solemnly, "Miss Sophy, if you deceive me, I shall scarce ever believe anyone again." Sophy answered with a smile, "You will never have reason for distrusting anyone. I shall never deceive you." Just before leaving, she assured him, "Of one thing, sir, be assured. I will never take any step in anything of importance without first consulting you."

But when Wesley called at the Caustons' home at ten o'clock

the next morning, Mrs. Causton told him, "Sir, Mr. Causton and I are exceedingly obliged to you for all the pains you have taken about Sophy. And so is Sophy too; and she desires you would publish the Banns of Marriage between her and Mr. Williamson on Sunday." Noticing Wesley's reaction, she said, "Sir, you don't seem to be well pleased. Have you any objection to it?" Wesley answered, "Madam, I don't seem to be awake. Surely I am in a dream." Mrs. Causton explained, "They agreed on it last night between themselves, after you was gone. And afterward Mr. Williamson asked Mr. Causton's and my consent, which we gave him. But if you have any objection to it, pray speak. Speak to her. . . . Go to her. She will be very glad to hear anything Mr. Wesley has to say. Pray go to her and talk with her yourself." But Wesley declined her suggestion, saying, "No, madam, if Miss Sophy is engaged, I have nothing to say. It will not signify for me to see her any more."

Later, Wesley described his thoughts upon hearing of Sophy's engagement.

> I doubted whether all this were not artifice, purely designed to quicken me and that as much engaged as she was, had I only said, "I am willing to marry her myself," that engagement would have vanished away. But though I was uneasy at the very mention of her marrying one who I believed would make her thoroughly miserable, yet I could not resolve to save her from him by marrying her myself. This was the only price I could not pay, and which therefore I never so much as hinted at in any of those following conversations wherein I so earnestly endeavoured to prevent that unhappy union.

Later that day, Wesley did talk with Sophy. Williamson was there when Wesley arrived. Williamson said, "I suppose, sir, you know what was agreed on last night between Miss Sophy and me?" Wesley answered, "I have heard something, but I could not believe it unless I should hear it from Miss Sophy herself." Sophy replied, "Sir, I have given Mr. Williamson my consent—unless you have anything to object." Wesley answered, "If you have given your consent, the time is past. I have nothing to object." Williamson left them alone for a time, during which little was said, "tears in both supplying the place of words."

About five o'clock that afternoon, Mr. Causton came to see Wesley and said, "I don't approve of this match. Mr. Williamson asked my consent this morning, but I have neither denied nor given it. Indeed I have often promised Sophy, so she would not have Mellichamp, she should have whom she would beside."

Causton then asked Wesley what had happened when he and Sophy talked that afternoon. Wesley described the conversation to him. Causton exclaimed, "If you loved her, how could you possibly be so overseen as not to press her, when she was so much moved? I will tell her my thoughts of it once more, and if you please, so may you. But if she is not then convinced, I must leave her to herself."

Wesley spoke with Sophy twice the next day, cautioning her about proceeding with her marriage plans, but never hinting that he had any thought of marrying her himself. On Friday morning, Sophy and Williamson left for South Carolina, and on Saturday they were married.

Wesley's anguish during these days is clearly revealed in his diary. The news of Sophy's engagement to Williamson brought him such distress as he had never known before.

> I came home and went into my garden. I walked up and down, seeking rest but finding none. From the beginning of my life to this hour, I had not known one such as this. God let loose my inordinate affection upon me, and the poison thereof drank up my spirit. I was as stupid as if but half awake, and yet in the sharpest pain I ever felt. "To see her no more!" That thought was the piercings of a sword. It was not to be borne—nor shaken off. I was weary of the world, of light, of life. Yet one way remained: to seek to God, a very present help in time of trouble. And I did seek after God, but I found him not. I forsook him before; now he forsook me. I could not pray. Then indeed the snares of death were about me; the pains of hell overtook me.

On the day that Sophia Hopkey was married, John Wesley wrote his will. Yet despite his own misery, the depth of his feeling for Sophy, his earnest conviction that her marriage to Williamson was a mistake, and all the obvious indications that both Sophy and the Caustons would have preferred that she marry Wesley, he persistently refused to propose marriage to her.

One recent writer, after describing Wesley's romance with Sophia Hopkey, summarized Wesley's attitude as follows.

> Theologically, in choosing between marriage and vocation, Wesley was choosing between a God who forgives shortcomings and uses earthen vessels, and a God who requires obedience and personal holiness as the price of his favor. It seems never to have occurred to Wesley that marriage might perfect vocation, just as God's forgiveness is the perfection of his sovereignty.[97]

While in Savannah, Wesley translated thirty-three hymns from *Das Gesang-Buch der Gemeine in Herrnhut*,[98] including Gerhard Ter-steegen's hymn, *Verborgne* [sic] *Gottes-Liebe du*. Wesley's translation of the fourth stanza of that hymn expresses the philosophy that guided Wesley at this point in his life, particularly in his relationship with Sophia Hopkey. We will bring this chapter to a close by quoting Wesley's translation of that stanza.

> Is there a thing beneath the sun
>   That strives with Thee my heart to share?
> Ah, tear it thence, that Thou alone
>   May'st reign unrivall'd Monarch there:
> From earthly loves I must be free
> Ere I can find repose in Thee.[99]

4

"Who Gyves Me This Wyfe?"

Parental Consent

The Tradition

ONE of the most perplexing changes that Wesley made in the marriage service was his elimination of the giving away of the bride, a practice that, according to Richard Hooker, could be traced back to ancient times. "All women which had not husbands nor fathers to govern them had their tutors, without whose authority there was no act which they did warrantable. And for this cause they were in marriage delivered unto their husbands by others."[1] In Anglo-Saxon weddings, after the espousals, all that was needed in order to complete the marriage was the giving away, in which the father physically placed the bride in the hands of her husband.[2] All editions of the prayer book from 1549 onward had required that the minister ask the question, "Who giveth this woman to be married to this man?" This question was derived from the medieval York liturgy, which required the minister to ask, "Who gyves me this wyfe?" The prayer book then states, "The Minister receiving the Woman at her Fathers or friends [sic] hands, shall cause the Man with his right hand, to take the woman by her right hand." With hands thus joined, the man and the woman then give to each other their wedding vows.[3]

Despite the change he was to make in the ceremony, John Wesley strongly agreed that Christians should not marry without the consent of their parents. He described the issue in economic terms in his comments on Genesis 2:24.

> See how necessary it is that children should take their parents [sic] consent with them in marriage; and how *unjust* they are to their parents, as well as *undutiful*, if they marry without it; for they *rob them* of their right to them, and interest in them, and alienate it to another fraudulently and unnaturally.[4]

During his career, Wesley had a number of opportunities to counsel people regarding parental consent in marriage. In 1767 he wrote to one woman that it would be best for her to marry, but he added, "I should scruple doing this without a parent's consent."[5] The following year, writing to a prospective bride, Wesley inquired if both she and her intended had the consent of their parents, for "without this there is seldom a blessing."[6] In 1781 Wesley wrote to one of his preachers named Elijah Bush and strongly cautioned him against marrying without parental consent.

> I was much concerned yesterday when I heard you were likely to marry a woman against the consent of your parents. I have never in an observation of fifty years known such a marriage attended with a blessing. I know not how it should be, since it is flatly contrary to the fifth commandment. I told my own mother, when pressing me to marry, "I dare not allow you a positive voice herein; I dare not marry a person because you bid me. But I must allow you a negative voice: I will marry no person if you forbid. I know it would be a sin against God." Take care what you do.[7]

In December 1787 Wesley wrote to a preacher name Thomas Roberts, and said that as long as both sets of parents were willing, he had no objection if Roberts wanted to marry.[8] But a month later, Wesley wrote again to offer his consolation.

> As the matter is now decided, I hope you are able to say, "Lord, not as I will, but as Thou wilt." I commend you for entirely giving up the matter when you found her parents were absolutely against it. I hope you will think of it no more, but will be now more unreservedly devoted to God than ever![9]

In Wesley's own family life we can find other examples of his insistence upon the importance of parental consent in marriage. In 1735 Westley Hall came to John Wesley and asked him to preside at Hall's marriage to Wesley's sister Patty that very morning. But Wesley advised Hall first to ask the consent of his own father and of Patty's uncle, John and Patty's father having recently died.[10] When Charles Wesley sought to marry Sally Gwynne in 1748–49, her mother was at first delighted with the prospect and exclaimed that she "would rather give her child to Mr. Wesley than to any man in England." But later she had reservations about Charles's ability to provide adequately for her daughter. The matter was resolved when John Wesley intervened and guaranteed in writing to provide Charles and Sally with a hundred pounds a year.[11]

Changing Times

Given Wesley's insistence, repeated so frequently throughout his life, that Christians ought not marry without the approval of their parents, why, then, did he eliminate from the wedding service the liturgical expression of that approval, namely, the giving away of the bride?

First of all, we should note that even Wesley allowed some exceptions to the rule about parental approval. The *Large Minutes* specified two situations in which a woman might marry against the wishes of her parents.

> Q. 20. Ought any woman to marry without the consent of her parents?
>
> A. In general she ought not. Yet there may be an exception. For if, (1.) A woman be under a necessity of marrying; if, (2.) Her parents absolutely refuse to let her marry any Christian; then she may, nay, ought to, marry without their consent. Yet, even then, a Methodist Preacher ought not to marry her.[12]

This paragraph was reproduced in the early American *Disciplines* with only minor changes in the wording.[13]

Secondly, like other English Protestant theologians, while he insisted on parental consent in most cases, Wesley also advised parents to be sensible.[14]

> As children ought not to marry without their parents [sic] consent, so parents ought not to marry them without their own. Before the matter is resolved on, ask at the damsel's mouth, she is a party principally concerned; and therefore ought to be principally consulted.[15]

We have already seen that in his own case, Wesley believed that his mother had the authority to forbid him to marry a particular person, but she could not *command* him to marry anyone (see page 81).

The spiritual welfare of their child should be the chief concern of the parents in considering a prospective marriage partner. "Parents, in disposing of their children, should carefully consult their futherance in the way to heaven."[16] Wesley was especially concerned about the number of parents who made decisions concerning a marriage partner for their child solely on the basis of financial considerations. Wesley emphasizes this point in his sermon "On Family Religion."

. . . if you are wise, you will not seek riches for your children by their marriage. See that your eye be single in this also: Aim simply at the glory of God, and the real happiness of your children, both in time and eternity. It is a melancholy thing to see how Christian parents rejoice in selling their son or their daughter to a wealthy Heathen! And do you seriously call this *a good match?* Thou fool, by parity of reason, thou mayest call hell *a good lodging,* and the devil *a good master.* O learn a better lesson from a better Master! "Seek ye first the kingdom of God and his righteousness," both for thyself and thy children: "and all other things shall be added unto you."[17]

Wesley does, therefore, place some limits on the authority of parents regarding the choice of a marriage partner for their children. But are these limitations adequate to explain Wesley's removal of the giving away of the bride from the wedding service, especially since he so strongly argues that, in most cases, children ought not marry without the approval of their parents? Probably not. Theological considerations alone are not enough to explain Wesley's actions; we gain a more comprehensive picture of the situation if we examine the changing social environment as well.

Between 1660 and 1800, marriages arranged by the parents gradually disappeared, and marriage by choice, with parental consent, became the norm. (This, of course, was the practice that Wesley, himself, supported.) Since the Puritan emphasis on marriage as a covenant of love was incompatible with marriage arranged by one's parents, nonconformists had led the way in demanding a free choice of marriage partners.[18] Only among the very rich and powerful did parents continue to select marriage partners for their children.[19]

Parents rarely attended the marriage ceremonies of their children. One historian describes the situation in this way.

The wedding itself was largely left to the peer group. Fathers did not usually give away their daughters; it was brothers or friends who accompanied the bride to church. Among the property holders, parental involvement was largely confined to the negotiations at the betrothal stage. As far as they were concerned, the marriage was complete once the portions and dowry had been arranged.[20]

John Wesley himself gave the bride away at a wedding he attended in 1759.[21] Charles Wesley notes in his description of his own wedding, "Mr. Gwynne gave her to me (under God)."[22] Had it been customary for the bride's father personally to take part in the wedding rite, it is less likely that Charles would have found

Mr. Gwynne's participation noteworthy. It is also pertinent to our present discussion to recall that the bride's mother was not among those whom Charles mentions as "all the persons present" at his wedding. (See page 45.) Mrs. Gwynne was not boycotting the wedding, since she is known to have approved of the marriage; she was simply following the social custom of the day, which gave her a central role in the financial arrangements, but neither required nor expected her presence at the wedding ceremony. By the time Wesley prepared the *Sunday Service* in 1784, "Less was made of the prenuputial formalities, and fathers seemed to have been much less involved at every stage of the marriage process."[23]

Another social reality that must be kept in mind is that nearly a third of all marriages ended by death within fifteen years. Twenty-five percent of all weddings were a remarriage for one of the partners.[24] Widows, of course, were not expected to seek parental approval, but were free to choose their own partners and contract their own marriages.[25] John Wesley himself intended to marry the widow Grace Murray and ultimately did marry another widow, Molly Vazeille. In neither case was there any male relative who needed to be consulted about the wedding plans.

This, then, was the situation at the time Wesley prepared the *Sunday Service*. Martin Bucer had said of the giving away of the bride, "It is declared by this rite that only those marriages should be consecrated in church which are contracted with the consent of the parents,"[26] but by the late eighteenth century, the giving away of the bride had ceased to signify any such thing, with the parents of the bride rarely even present for the wedding, as we have seen. In the case of widows, parental consent was not even required. And even Wesley had to acknowledge that, in some cases, it was better to marry against the wishes of one's parents. Unfortunately, we have no statement from Wesley himself regarding the giving away of the bride, so we can only speculate as to why he eliminated this part of the marriage liturgy. But given what we know about the wedding customs of the day, we can only conclude that Wesley must have felt the giving away of the bride had become superfluous.

Choosing a Partner

The Role of Providence

The new freedom of choosing one's own marriage partner brought with it the responsibility of choosing wisely. As Wesley himself discovered, even persons who intend to remain single cannot be sure they will not some day face the responsibility of making such a choice.

A clear conviction of the superior advantages of a single life certainly implies a call from God to abide therein; supposing a person has received that gift from God. But we know, all cannot receive this saying: And I think, none ought to make any vows concerning it; because, although we know what we are, and what we can do now, yet we do not know what we shall be.[27]

Any decision to alter one's marital status ought to be made very cautiously.

You have some thoughts of altering your condition; and we know, "marriage is honourable in all men." But is your eye single herein? This is worthy of your most serious consideration. Retire a little into yourself, and ask your own heart: "What is it moves me to think of this?"[28]

In 1778 Wesley wrote to one of his preachers that he had no objection to the woman the preacher intended to marry, but he advised, "Whatever you do should be done with much prayer, as the matter is of no small importance."[29] In his comments on 1 Corinthians 7:20, Wesley observed that no one should seek to change his marital status "without a clear direction from Providence."[30]

For Wesley, the marriages of Isaac and Rebekah and Jacob and Rachel were prime examples of how God providentially brings people together. It was no coincidence that Isaac and Rebekah found each other.

We have here the making up of the marriage between *Isaac* and *Rebekah*, related largely and particularly. Thus, we are directed to take notice of God's providence in the little common occurrences of human life, and in them also to exercise our own prudence, and other graces: for the scripture was not intended only for the use of philosophers and statesmen, but to make us all wise and virtuous in the conduct of ourselves and families.[31]

The meeting of Jacob and Rachel in Genesis 29 gave Wesley an opportunity to further elaborate upon this point.

Providence brought him to the very field where his uncle's flocks were to be watered, and there he met with *Rachel* that was to be his wife.

The Divine Providence is to be acknowledged in all the little circumstances which concur to make a journey or other undertaking comfortable and successful. If, when we are at a loss, we meet with those seasonably that can direct us; if we meet with a disaster, and those are at hand that will help us; we must not say it was by chance, but it was by providence; our ways are ways of pleasantness, if we continually acknowledge God in them.[32]

And when Wesley came to the proverb that says, "Whoso findeth a wife findeth a good thing," he was moved to comment that the finder of a good wife "obtains her not by his own diligence, but by God's good providence."[33]

In his own personal life, Wesley faithfully adhered to the principles he laid down for others. It will be remembered that when he was utterly at a loss as to how to proceed in his relationship with Sophia Hopkey, he sought divine guidance by drawing lots (see page 76). In his journal, Wesley affirmed his conviction that God had, in fact, directed him through this means.

From the direction I received from God this day touching an affair of the greatest importance, I could not but observe (as I had done many times before) the entire mistake of those who assert, "God will not answer your prayer unless your heart be wholly resigned to his will." My heart was not wholly resigned to his will. Therefore, not daring to depend on my own judgment, I cried the more earnestly to him to supply what was wanting in me. And I know, and am assured, he heard my voice and did sent forth his light and his truth.[34]

And when Grace Murray married John Bennet, Wesley, even through his grief and tears, affirmed that this, too, had been the work of God. Like Job before him, Wesley struggled to make sense of this cruel turn of events.

Unsearchable they Judgments are,
O Lord, a bottomless Abyss!
Yet sure thy Love, thy guardian Care,
O'er all thy Works extended is.
O why didst thou the Blessing send?
Or why thus snatch away my Friend?[35]

But even the most earnest seeker after God's will may sometimes be mistaken. Charles Wesley records that two weeks after John Wesley's marriage, John publicly stated, "I am no more sure that God sent His Son into the world than that it is His will I should marry."[36] But years later, John Wesley himself cautioned against using such an expression.

> So one says, "I am as sure this is the will of God, as that I am justified." Another says, "God as surely spake this to my heart as ever he spoke to me at all." This is an exceedingly dangerous way of thinking or speaking. We know not what it may lead us to. It may sap the very foundation of our religion. It may insensibly draw us into Deism or Atheism. My dear Nancy, my sister, my friend, beware of this![37]

Such expressions are dangerous not only because they presume to know too much about the mind of God, but also because, if we should happen to be mistaken about God's guidance, we may be led to doubt even our salvation. Only the scriptures are an unimpeachable source of guidance. This is the point Wesley emphasized to one of his female correspondents.

> . . . you will be the better enabled, by your own experience, to guard all, especially young persons, from laying stress upon anything but the written word of God. Guard them against reasoning in that dangerous manner, "If I was deceived in this, then I was deceived in thinking myself justified." Not at all; although nature, or Satan in the latter case, admirably well mimicked the works of God.[38]

Marriage with Unbelievers

But there are some matters on which it is not necessary to seek God's direction because the question has already been clearly resolved by the teaching of holy writ. The marriage of a Christian and an unbeliever is one example of an issue about which there could be no doubt.

> Above all, we should tremble at the very thought of entering into a marriage-covenant, the closest of all others, with any person who does not love or at least fear God. This is the most horrid folly, the most deplorable madness, that a child of God could possibly plunge into; as it implies every sort of connexion with the ungodly which a Christian is bound in conscience to avoid. No wonder, then, it is so flatly forbidden of God; that the prohibition is so absolute and peremptory: "Be not unequally yoked with an unbeliever." Nothing can be more express.[39]

Wesley found support for his contention that such marriages are contrary to the will of God in the Old Testament as well as in the New. Deuteronomy 7:1–4 prohibits marriage between the

Israelites and other nations. Wesley explains that "there is manifest danger of apostacy and idolatry from such matches." When
Ruth 1:3–4 says that Naomi's sons married Moabite women, Wesley concludes, "Either these were Proselytes when they married
them, or they sinned in marrying them, and therefore were pun-
ished with short life, and want of issue." And the exhortation in
Ezra 9:12 about the danger of marrying foreigners is paraphrased
by Wesley in this way: "Although you may fancy that making
leagues and marriages with them is the only way to establish
you, yet I assure you, it will weaken and ruin you, and the contrary course will make you strong."[40]

When Paul states in 1 Corinthians 7:39 that a widow is free to
marry whomever she wills "only in the Lord," Wesley explains
that this means, "Only let Christians marry Christians: a standing
direction, and one of the utmost importance." And Wesley said
that the teaching of the Apostle about being "unequally yoked
with unbelievers" applies to "Christians with Jews or heathens.
The apostle particularly speaks of marriage. But the reasons he
urges equally hold against any needless intimacy with them."[41]

The Large Minutes required that any Methodist who married
an unbeliever be expelled.

> Q. 18. Do we observe any evil which has lately prevailed among
> our societies?
>
> A. Many of our members have married with unbelievers, yea, with
> unawakened persons. This has had fatal effects. They had either a
> cross for life, or turned back to perdition.
>
> Q. 19. What can be done to put a stop to this?
>
> A. (1.) Let every Preacher publicly enforce the Apostle's caution,
> "Be not unequally yoked with unbelievers." (2.) Let him openly de-
> clare, whoever does this will be expelled the society. (3.) When any
> such is expelled, let a suitable exhortation be subjoined. And, (4.) Let
> all be exhorted to take no step in so weighty a matter without advising
> with the most serious of their brethren.[42]

Wesley did acknowledge, however, that there were cases in
which unbelievers had been brought to faith through the influence of a Christian spouse. Commenting on 1 Corinthians 7:14,
Wesley wrote, "For the unbelieving husband hath, in many instances,
been sanctified by the wife." He also pointed out that, were it not
for the faith of the believing parent, the children of such unions
"would have been brought up heathens; whereas now they are
Christians."[43]

Wesley, in his correspondence, frequently had occasion to warn people of the dangers of marrying someone who did not share their faith. In a letter written in 1768, he is clear about the questions one should ask concerning a prospective marriage partner.

Is the person a believer? Is he a Methodist? Is he a member of our Society? Is he clear with regard to the doctrine of Perfection? Is he athirst for it? If he fails in any of these particulars, I fear he would be an hindrance to you rather than a help.[44]

In 1771 Wesley wrote to a man named Thomas Mason and urged him not to go through with his marriage plans because, not only was his intended too young for him, but "she has only little if any Christian experience."[45] And in 1774 Wesley wrote frankly to his friend Ann Bolton about the man she intended to marry.

He has neither such a measure of understanding nor of spiritual experience as to advance you either in divine knowledge or in the life of God. Therefore yield to no importunity, and be as peremptory as you can consistent with civility. This is the wisest way with regard for you and the kindest with regard to him.[46]

The marriage plans were eventually canceled (though apparently not because of Wesley's advice), and Wesley wrote again to Ann Bolton, rebuking her for her reaction to the broken engagement.

God has lately delivered you out of imminent danger, that of being unequally yoked with an unbeliever. . . .
And now, instead of praising God for your great deliverance, you are against Him, as [if] it were no deliverance at all! You are fretting and grieving yourself because the snare is broken, because your soul is taken out of the net! But must not this grieve the Holy Spirit of God? What deep unthankfulness! . . . You have acted wisely and faithfully. God has heard your prayer. He is well pleased with the sacrifice you have made. [Admit] no thought to the contrary; and if one should, give no place to it—no, not for a moment.[47]

In 1789 Wesley wrote to Jane Bisson to say that even though her new husband was only "a babe in Christ," it was no sin to marry him.

If you had married an ungodly man, it would certainly have been a sin. But it was no sin to marry a child of God; yea, though he were but a babe in Christ. And surely, if you pray mightily for him, the

Lord will hear your prayer, and supply whatever is yet wanting in his faith, till he is happy.[48]

Testing the Choice

Wesley recognized that during courtship, the parties are trying to please each other and so are on their best behavior. But after marriage, they sometimes show a less attractive side of themselves that they had hidden earlier. Proverbs 30:23 says that "an odious woman when she is married" disquiets the earth. Wesley explains that this is because "then she displays all those ill humours, which before she concealed."[49]

Wesley specifically warned against falling prey to the charms of physical beauty. Proverbs 31:30 warns, "Favour is deceitful, and beauty is vain," and Wesley, in his *Notes*, explains the danger of this deception.

> It gives a false representation of the person, being often a cover to a deformed soul; it does not give a man that satisfaction, which at first he promised to himself from it; and it is soon lost, not only by death, but by many diseases and contingences.[50]

Wesley was evidently not the only Englishman who was concerned about the deception of physical appearance. For in 1770 Parliament had passed a law which made it illegal for a woman to use any perfume, cosmetics, wigs, or other beauty aids as a means of enticing a man into marriage.

> All women, of whatever age, rank, profession, or degree, whether virgins, maids, or widows, that shall, from and after such Act, impose upon, seduce, or betray into matrimony, any of his Majesty's male subjects by the scents, paints, cosmetic washes, artificial teeth, false hair, Spanish wool, iron stays, hoops, high-heeled shoes, etc., shall incur the penalty of the law now enforced against witchcraft and like misdemeanours, and that the marriage upon conviction shall stand null and void.[51]

One means of avoiding such deception was to marry only after a long acquaintance with a person. One of the reasons Wesley felt so confident that Grace Murray would be a good wife was that she had lived in his household for so many years.

> By living so long with her under one Roof, I am as secure against being deceived in her, as I can well be against being deceived in any

one. Indeed I should scruple marrying any Woman, who had not done so for some time.[52]

In fact, so careful was Wesley in approaching marriage with Grace Murray that he actually sought out "all those who were disgusted at her, and inquired into their Reasons for it."[53] After listening to those who spoke ill of Grace, Wesley concluded that their criticisms were unfounded.

I plainly perceived Jealousy and Envy were the real ground of most of these Accusations: And idle, senseless Prejudice, of the rest. Offence taken, but not given. So that, after all, her Character appeared untouched, and for any thing they could prove, She had done all things well.[54]

Consultation with others was, for Wesley, an important means by which Christians could avoid making a mistake in their choice of a marriage partner. The journal of Charles Wesley shows that he scrupulously adhered to this rule in making his own marriage plans.

My brother and I having promised each other, (as soon as he came from Georgia), that we would neither of us marry, or take any step toward it, without the other's knowledge and consent, to-day I fairly and fully communicated every thought of my heart. He had proposed three persons to me, S.P., M.W., and S.G., and entirely approved my choice of the last. We consulted together about every particular, and were of one heart and mind in all things.[55]

John Wesley likewise sought the approval of Charles upon his plans to marry Grace Murray, but with less happy results. Yet even so, when John heard the objections that Charles raised to the proposed union, he considered his brother's viewpoint carefully.

As soon as I was alone, I began to consider with myself, Whether I was *in my Senses*, or no? Whether Love had *put out my Eyes* (as my Brother affirmed) or I had the use of them still? I weighed the Steps I had taken, yet again, and the grounds on which I had proceeded.[56]

But after reviewing the matter once again, Wesley concluded that his brother was mistaken.[57] Probably because of Charles's interference in John's marriage plans with Grace Murray, when John decided to marry Molly Vazeille, he *told*, rather than *asked* Charles about his intentions, and he did not even tell Charles who the bride was to be! John did, however, consult his trusted friend Vincent Perronet who advised Wesley to marry.[58]

The principle of consulting others before proceeding with marriage plans was eventually codified in the Large Minutes, which, as we have already noted, required of Methodist preachers that they "take no step toward marriage, without first consulting your brethren" (see page 70). Wesley also regarded it as part of his pastoral responsibility to advise persons not to proceed with marriage plans which he regarded as mistaken. While in Savannah, Wesley tried to persuade Miss Sophy's friend, Miss Bovey, that the man she intended to marry was not a good choice for her. Wesley recorded, "Though we did not entirely agree in our judgment, she took it as it was intended."[59]

As we have seen in the excerpts from Wesley's correspondence which have already been quoted, Wesley was not shy about giving his advice, solicited or unsolicited, regarding marriage plans. However, when that advice was not heeded, Wesley still sought to maintain a supportive relationship with the person. We see an example of this in a 1783 letter to a woman named Ann Loxdale in which Wesley promised to say nothing further against a marriage of which he strongly disapproved.

> Because I loved you, and because I thought it my duty, I wrote freely to you on a tender point. But I have done. I do not know that I shall speak one word more concerning it. The regard which I have for you will not suffer me to give you any pain which answers no good purpose. So you may still think him as holy as Thomas Walsh; I will say nothing against it.[60]

The Wedding Ring

Origin of the Ring Ceremony

As we have seen, in the late Middle Ages the giving of a ring was part of the "espousals," the ceremony in which a man and a woman promised to marry one another (see page 15). The inclusion of the ring as part of the espousals seems to have been derived from the early Anglo-Saxon custom of the groom and his family giving to the bride's family a series of "weds": sureties given as a guarantee that the bride would be properly maintained by her future husband.[61]

The medieval Sarum rite included the giving of a ring as part of the marriage service at the church door. The Sarum manual directed that as the man gave the ring to the woman, he was to say, "With this rynge I the wed, and this gold and siluer I the geue, and with my body I the worshipe, and with all my worldely [sic] cathel I the endowe. *In nomine Patris et Filii et Spiritus sancti. Amen."* As the groom said, "in the name of the Father," he was to slip the ring over the bride's thumb; at the mention of the Son, the ring was moved to the index finger; the name of the Holy Spirit brought the ring to the third finger, and at the word "amen," the ring was placed on the fourth finger, where it remained. The ring was left on the fourth finger because it was believed that a vein in that finger ran directly to the heart.[62] In medieval England, it was customary for the woman to wear the ring on her *right* hand.[63]

The 1549 Book of Common Prayer says that "the man shal geue vnto the woman a ring, and other tokens of spousage, as gold or silver, laying the same vpon the booke."[64] The prayer book specified that the ring was to be placed on the fourth finger of the woman's *left* hand. The wearing of one's wedding ring on the left hand was becoming more popular in sixteenth-century Europe. It is possible that this was because of the influence of Renaissance writers who said that ancient people wore their rings on the left hand.[65] There is no mention of moving the ring from finger to finger. The words said at the giving of the ring are almost an exact duplication of the Sarum liturgy, except that "worldely cathel" has become "worldly goodes" and the Trinitarian formula is said in English rather than Latin.[66]

There were some changes in the ring ceremony in the 1552 edition of the prayer book. The reference to "other tokens of spousage, as gold or siluer" disappeared from the rubric, as did the words in the text, "This golde and siluer I thee geue," repeated by the man as the ring is given. The 1552 prayer book also specified that the man is to lay the ring on the priest's book "with the accustomed duty to the priest and clerke."[67] Paying the clergy their fee has actually become part of the liturgy!

The ring ceremony in the 1662 prayer book is the same as the 1552 service with only two exceptions. The man is directed to place the ring upon the fourth finger of the woman's left hand and to *hold it there* as he repeats the words after the priest. Thus, the custom of moving the ring from finger to finger is explicitly repudiated. The 1662 prayer book also specifies that the couple is to kneel for prayer following the giving of the ring.[68]

Puritan Objections

The Continental reformer Martin Bucer, in his 1551 *Censura*, a critical examination of the new Anglican rites, approved of the giving of a ring in matrimony, especially since the prayer book specified that the ring was first to be placed on the priest's book, and then returned to the man to be given to the woman. Bucer saw a symbolic significance in this action.

> We might regard this as a very suitable rite if at the same time its significance was explained to the people.
> The explanation would be of this kind. First, that the ring and other gifts with which the bridegroom wishes to adorn the bride are first placed on the holy book and then returned by the minister to the bridegroom to be given to the bride: this signifies that we ought to offer and consecrate all things to God, to whom they belong, before we use them, and receive them as if it were from his hand and use them to his glory.
> Secondly, that the ring is placed on the finger next to the small finger of the left hand, in which finger, they say, a vein runs from the heart to finish here and unite with other veins in the finger: this signifies that the heart of the bride ought always to be bound to her husband with the bond of love, a bond which must have no end just as the ring has no end.[69]

But Bucer's approval of the ring ceremony is qualified. He does not object to the ring ceremony itself; indeed, he regards it as "very suitable," *if* "at the same time its significance was explained to the people." Bucer is apparently concerned lest the ring be regarded as a sacramental sign like the water in baptism and the bread in the Eucharist and be granted more significance than simply as a token of matrimony.

Other writers were not willing to grant even qualified approval to the wedding ring. In 1572 the Puritan *Admonition to Parliament* was published. This pamphlet included a section called "A View of Popishe Abuses Yet Remaining in the Englishe Church." It described in blunt language the Puritan objections to the Book of Common Prayer, which, according to the Puritans, had been "culled and picked out of that popishe dunghill, the Masse booke full of all abhominations."[70] The Anglican marriage service was no more able than other parts of the prayer book to escape the Puritan ax, and the ring ceremony was especially held up as an object of scorn.

As for matrimony, that also hath corruptions, too many. It was wont to be called a sacrament, and therefore they use yet a sacramental sign to which they attribute the virtue of wedlock. I mean the wedding ring, which they foully abuse and dally withal in taking it up and laying it down. In putting it on they abuse the name of the Trinity; they make the new-married man, according to the popish form, to make an idol of his wife, saying "With this ring I thee wed, and with my body I thee worship."[71]

John Whitgift, the Archbishop of Canterbury, attempted to answer the Puritan objections. Whitgift argued that the ring could not be construed as a sacramental sign because it was not even necessary in matrimony. Whitgift quoted Bucer's words in support of the ring ceremony.[72] Whitgift also argued that not only were the words "With my body I thee worship" not idolatrous, but that nobody would be so foolish as to think that the husband, in saying these words, was ascribing to his wife a reverence that was due only to God. In this context, the word "worship" meant the same thing as the word "honour" in 1 Peter 3:7, which teaches, "Likewise, ye husbands, dwell with them according to knowledge, giving honour unto the wife."[73]

But the Puritans responded that, in spite of Bucer's teaching, to institute any new signs or sacraments was both dangerous and unlawful, "especially in this which confirmeth the false and popish opinion of a sacrament." It was "very ridiculous" to find allegorical meanings in the shape of the ring, the act of placing the ring on the book, and the supposed vein that runs from the ring finger to the heart. And finally, "that he will have the minister to preach upon these toys, surely it savoureth not of the learning and sharpness of the judgment of M. Bucer."[74]

The Millenary Petition, a statement of Puritan concerns addressed to James I in 1603, asked that the ring be deleted from the marriage ceremony.[75] At the Hampton Court Conference summoned by the king to discuss these concerns, King James himself attempted to persuade the Puritans that "worship," in this context, meant "to honor." The king is reported to have told Dr. Reynolds, the Puritan spokesman, "If you had a good wife yourself, you would think all the honor and worship you could do to her well bestowed."[76]

When the Puritans came to power under Oliver Cromwell, their liturgical manual, *The Westminster Directory*, like the 1562 *Book of Common Order* of the Church of Scotland, included no ring ceremony as part of the wedding rite.[77] At the Savoy Conference of

1661, the Puritans repeated their objections to the use of the ring and the words, "With my body I thee worship,"[78] but both the giving of the ring and the objectionable words were retained in the 1662 edition of the Book of Common Prayer.

Wesley and the Ring

John Wesley, however, eliminated any mention of a wedding ring from the marriage liturgy in the *Sunday Service*. Most writers have attributed Wesley's action to Puritan influence.[79] The only other hypothesis that has been published regarding Wesley's deletion of the ring ceremony appeared in the United Methodist *A Service of Christian Marriage*, first published in 1979. This material was later reprinted in the *Companion to "The Book of Services"*. There it states that Wesley omitted the ring ceremony, "perhaps because of scruples about wearing ornaments and jewels," but no evidence is offered in support of this suggestion.[80] In 1995, Karen Westerfield Tucker explained the charitable motive behind Wesley's objections to jewelry.

> Concern for the poor may have also been an underlying motivation for Wesley's deletion of the wedding ring from "The Form of Solemnization of Matrimony"; the purchase money used for the wedding ring, as with other superfluous ostentation condemned by the Methodist societies, was best used in the care of the needy.[81]

In his article, "Advice to the People Called Methodists with Regard to Dress," Wesley wrote, "I do not advise women to wear rings," and the General Rules of the Methodist Societies prohibited "the putting on of gold and costly apparel." Furthermore, members of "band-societies" (small groups of believers who met together regularly to encourage each other and pray for one another) were told "to wear no needless ornaments, such as rings, ear-rings, necklaces, lace, ruffles."[82]

Certainly, Wesley's concerns about jewelry must have figured in his decision to omit the giving of a ring from the marriage ceremony. But what was Wesley's position regarding the debate between Puritans and Anglicans over the use of the ring?

In his address to the Methodist Conference of 1755, in which he lists those portions of the prayer book to which he could not give assent, no mention is made of the wedding ring, nor is such a complaint found elsewhere in any of his extant writings.

We know that Wesley regarded certain liturgical questions as matters of indifference. He attributed disputes over such matters to misguided zeal.

> Who were men of stronger understandings than Bishop Ridley and Bishop Hooper? And how warmly did these, and other great men of that age, dispute about the *sacerdotal vestments!* How eager was the contention for almost a hundred years, for and against wearing a *surplice!* O shame to man! I would as soon have disputed about a straw or a barley-corn![83]

We also know that Wesley intended the *Sunday Service* to be flexible enough to fit the various circumstances in which Methodist preachers in North America found themselves. To that end, Wesley deleted all references to such indifferent matters as church architecture and clerical vestments (see pages 44–45). Despite his strong stand on issues of importance to him, Wesley was prepared to compromise on matters that did not violate his principles.

A case in point is the matter of kneeling to receive communion. The Puritans had long objected to the Anglican practice of kneeling for communion, fearing that such a posture implied adoration of the consecrated elements. A rubric that appeared in the 1552 and the 1662 editions of the prayer book explaining that kneeling was in no way intended to suggest adoration of the elements did little to assuage their concerns. Although Wesley himself strongly preferred to receive communion "meekly kneeling," as the prayer book required, he removed those words from the communion liturgy in the *Sunday Service*.[84] The early American Methodist *Disciplines* perpetuated Wesley's example of accommodation.

> *Quest.* Are there any directions to be given concerning the administration of the Lord's supper?
> *Answ.* 1. Let those who have scruples concerning the receiving of it kneeling, be permitted to receive it either standing or sitting.[85]

Even the use of the *Sunday Service* itself was not a point for which Wesley was willing to fight. Wesley encouraged the use of his revised version of the prayer book in England as well as in America, but he instructed his preachers, "Wherever the people make an objection, let the matter drop." It was apparently because some of his followers objected to the *Sunday Service* that Wesley himself continued to use the Book of Common Prayer at City Road Chapel in London.[86]

This same principle was probably guiding Wesley in regard to the wedding ring. Because orthodox Anglican theology taught that the ring was not essential to matrimony, and because Wesley wanted the *Sunday Service* to be as flexible and practical as possible for the American Methodists, it seemed to him that the most prudent course was to eliminate the giving of the ring.

5

"The Holy Estate of Matrimony"

Directions for Married Persons

THERE is one article which was not written by Wesley, but which may be taken as reliably representing his own opinion. William Whateley (sometimes spelled "Whatley") was a Puritan minister who, in 1617, published *A Bride-Bush or, A Direction for Married Persons. Plainely Describing the Duties Common to both, and particularly to each of them.*[1] Wesley reprinted Whateley's article twice in his own publications and he gave it his highest recommendation. He wrote of it, "I am persuaded, it is not possible for me to write anything so full, so strong, and so clear on this subject, as has been written near an hundred and fifty years ago, by a person of equal sense and piety."[2] He also said,

> I have seen nothing on the subject in any either ancient or modern tongue which is in any degree comparable to it;—it is so full, so deep, so closely, so strongly written, and yet with the most exquisite decency, even where the author touches on points of the most delicate nature that are to be found within the whole compass of divinity. I cannot therefore but earnestly recommend it to the most serious and attentive consideration of all those married persons, who desire to have a conscience void of offence, and to adorn the gospel of God our Saviour.[3]

Wesley recommended the *Directions for Married Persons* (for this was the title he used for it) not only to husbands and wives, but also to couples about to be married, as can be seen in this excerpt from a letter to a woman named Ellen Gretton who was about to marry a man named William Christian.

> It might be of use for Mr. Christian and you carefully to read over and consider those Directions to Married Persons which are in the fourth volume of *Sermons*. Whatever family follows those directions will be as a city set upon a hill.[4]

In addition to including it with a collection of his sermons, Wesley also printed Whateley's article in *A Christian Library,* an anthology of fifty volumes which Wesley prepared between 1749 and 1755.[5] We will refer to Whateley's essay a number of times as we consider John Wesley's ideas about married life.

The Family Hierarchy

Spiritual Equality and Mutual Dependence

In several places in his writings, John Wesley emphasizes the spiritual equality of man and woman. Underlying their differences in physique, temperament, and social role is an essential unity. This essential unity is stated in Wesley's comments on the creation of woman in Genesis 2:23: ". . . she shall be called *woman, Isha,* a *She-man,* differing from man in sex only, not in nature; made *of man,* and joined *to man."*[6] The essential unity of man and woman is assumed by Wesley when he uses that unity in an allegorical description of the unity between God and Christ.

> Christ, as he is Mediator, acts in all things subordinately to his Father. But we can no more infer that they are not of the same divine nature, because God is said to be *the head of Christ,* than that man and woman are not of the same human nature, because the man is said to be *the head of the woman.*[7]

Neither sex can get along without the other; both Adam and Eve were created as single parts of a larger whole.

> Therefore Adam did not at first contain both sexes in himself; but God made Adam, when first created, male only; and Eve female only. And this man and woman he joined together, in a state of innocence, as husband and wife.[8]

Wesley's comments upon 1 Corinthians 11:12 make this divinely ordained interdependence even more clear.

> *And as the woman was* at first taken out *of the man, so also the man is* now, in the ordinary course of nature, *by the woman; but all things are of God*—The man, the woman, and their dependence on each other.[9]

Spiritually, man and woman are absolutely equal; in commenting on 1 Corinthians 11:11, Wesley said, *"Nevertheless in the Lord Jesus, there is neither male nor female*—Neither is excluded; neither is preferred before the other in his kingdom."[10] This is true regardless of the "weaknesses" traditionally attributed to the female sex.

> *Dwell with the woman according to knowledge*—Knowing they are weak, and therefore to be used with all tenderness. Yet do not despise them for this, but *give them honour*—Both in heart, in word, and in action; *as* those who are called to be *joint-heirs of* that eternal *life* which ye and they hope to receive by the free *grace of* God.[11]

This spiritual equality meant that women were capable of some surprisingly "masculine" accomplishments. In contrast to his contemporaries, Wesley not only admitted women to religious societies, but put them in positions of leadership.[12] Wesley's own mother had, of course, provided him with a striking example of the important leadership role that woman can play in the Christian community. Perhaps Wesley had her in mind when he made this point in his *Explanatory Notes upon the Old Testament*.

> Souls know no difference of sex: many a manly heart is lodged in a female breast. Nor is the treasure of wisdom the less valuable, for being lodged in the weaker vessel.[13]

The Obedience of the Wife

But in spite of Wesley's comments about the spiritual equality of man and woman, he also believed firmly in the divinely ordained subordination of women to their husbands. With the exception of the closing homily, which he omitted entirely (see pages 46–47), Wesley retained all three of the phrases in the prayer book wedding service which mention the obedience of the wife to her husband.

The first of these occurs in the espousals, which require the woman's consent to the question, "Wilt thou obey him, and serve him?" This question came from the medieval Sarum rite (*ei obedire & servire*) and had appeared in every edition of the prayer book since 1549.[14]

The bride's wedding vow itself included a promise to obey, which had also appeared in all editions of the prayer book. This promise was a revision of the more picturesque language of the Sarum rite, in which the bride promised "to be bonere and buxum in bedde and at te borde."[15]

The third reference to the wife's obedience is in the closing prayer, which asks "that this woman may be loving and amiable, faithful and obedient to her husband." This prayer also originated in the Sarum rite; however, the words "faithful and obedient" were not inserted until 1662.[16]

Wesley regarded the subordination of women as a punishment for Eve's sin, not as God's original intention in creation. Wesley explains this in his comments on Genesis 3:16.

> We have here the sentence past upon *the woman*; she is condemned to a state of *sorrow* and a state of *subjection*: proper punishments of a sin in which she had gratified her *pleasure* and her *pride*. . . . the whole sex, which by creation was equal with man, is for sin made inferior.[17]

Wesley frequently commented on the subordination of women in his biblical *Notes*. The husband is the "governor, guide, and guardian of the wife." Wives are told to give their husbands "that entire submission that soldiers pay to their general." And he observed that "Meek submission to their husbands" was characteristic of "holy women, who trusted in God."[18]

William Whateley, in *Directions for Married Persons*, was equally clear about the divinely ordained family hierarchy. Whateley said, "The man must be taken for God's immediate officer in the house, and as it were the king in the family; the woman must account herself his deputy, an officer substituted to him, not as equal, but as subordinate."[19] This divinely ordained hierarchy applied even though a particular woman might be far more intelligent, skilled, and capable than her husband.

> Let us grant, that in gifts thou art his better, having more wit and understanding, more readiness of speech, more dexterity in managing affairs, and whatsoever other good quality may be incident to a woman; yet understand, that so may thy servant exceed thee as much as thou dost him. Hath not many a servant more wit and understanding, and often more grace too, than master and mistress put together? Yet loth would the wife be, that the servant should deny both to her husband and herself the name of Betters. Know, then, that a man may be superior in place to one to whom he is inferior in gifts; and know also, that thou dost abuse the good parts which God hath given thee, in seeking thence to infringe thine husband's superiority.[20]

According to Wesley, wives are permitted to disobey their husbands only if obedience to one's husband would require disobedience to God. In 1737 Wesley had given this instruction to Sophia

Hopkey after her marriage to William Williamson: "In things of an indifferent nature you cannot be too obedient to your husband; but if his will should be contrary to the will of God, you are to obey God rather than man."[21]

Commenting on Ephesians 5:22, Wesley wrote *"Wives, submit yourselves to your own husbands*—Unless where God forbids. Otherwise, in all indifferent things, the will of the husband is a law to the wife." Wives are to obey their husbands in everything "which is not contrary to any command of God." Wesley wrote that "in all things lawful," the will of the husband "is a rule to the wife."[22]

William Whateley had likewise written, "In whatever matter a woman's yielding to her husband will not provoke a rebellion against her Maker, in that matter she is bound in conscience to yield unto him, without any further question."[23]

The Duties of the Husband

But Wesley also retained in the *Sunday Service* the words from the prayer book that speak of the husband loving the wife "as Christ did love his spouse the Church, who gave himself for it; loving and cherishing it, even as his own flesh." He was again reflecting the thought of William Whateley, who, in the *Directions for Married Persons*, discussed at some length the duties incumbent upon the Christian husband. Whateley wrote that husbands dishonor God by abdicating the leadership role that God had placed in their hands and allowing their wives to rule the family.

> No general would thank a captain for surrendering his place to some common soldier, nor will God an husband, for suffering his wife to bear the sway. It is dishonourable to the prince, if subordinate officers yield the honour of their places to meaner subjects; and the contempt rebounds upon God, which a man is willing to take upon himself, by making his wife his master.[24]

But this does not mean the husband is to be a tyrant. Rather, the husband is to maintain his authority by being such a model of virtue that his wife cannot help but respect him.

> Know ye, therefore, all ye husbands, that the way to maintain authority is, not to use violence, but skill. Not by main force must an husband hold his own right against his wife's undutifulness, but by a more mild, gentle, and wise proceeding. We wish not any man to use big looks, great words, and a fierce behaviour, but we advise you to

a more easy and certain course. Let the husband endeavour to gain all commendable virtues, and to exceed his wife as much in goodness as he doth in place. Let his wife see in him such humility, such godliness, such wisdom, as may cause her heart to confess, that there is in him something that deserveth to be stooped to. Let him walk uprightly, christianly, soberly, religiously, in his family, and give a good example to all in the household; then shall the wife willingly give him the better place, when she cannot but see him to be the better person.[25]

Whateley wrote that the purpose of the husband's authority is the welfare of the wife, *not* the husband's own ease and comfort. The husband must never command the wife to do anything contrary to the laws of God or the magistrates, nor may he command her to act contrary to her own conscience. Husbands must not find fault with their wives where no fault exists, nor may they reprove a wife for a fault she has already corrected.[26] A man may punish his wife by treating her coolly, but he should do so only as a last resort.

For a man to estrange his countenance and behaviour toward his wife, to withdraw the testimonies of his love, or to cease to trust her and speak familiarly and cheerfully to her; these are such things as deserve the name of chastisements. The wife that hath not forgotten all good affection to her husband, cannot but smart and bleed under these stripes, as I may call them. They are therefore to be of rare use, and not applied at all, till the grossness of much misdemeanour shall compel.[27]

Husbands should also remember not only to correct the faults of their wives, but to be lavish in praising them. And when correction is necessary, husbands should be careful to choose the proper time and place to speak to their wives. Husbands should not offer corrections when they are angry, or when their wives' health or frame of mind might hinder their receptivity.[28] And while husbands should praise their wives in the presence of others, they must be careful to criticize only in private. "Wherefore if any thing be amiss, whereof thou wouldst admonish thy wife, take her aside, and let her hear it from thee, when she is well assured that no ear shall be privy to thy words but her own."[29]

Whateley also dealt with the issue of how a husband should respond if a wife should take advantage of his unwillingness to correct her in public.

It may be objected, That some women will not fear to offend in public, before the servants and children, and strangers; and if the husband then forbear to speak to her, and let her go away with it so, would not this prove infectious to the beholders, and make them apt to follow the same trade of evil doing? I answer, if such public faults fall out, a man may shew his dislike in a patient manner of speaking, and make it appear that he doth not wink at his wife's faults. But I answer again, that in such a case he must express grief rather than anger, and must defer the lawful sharpness, and (as I may call it) wholesome lancing, by a reproof, till his wife and himself be together alone; and by that time she will remember how she overshot herself, if he give her not the advantage of replying, by being carried into some absurdity with her for company.[30]

Whateley wrote that husbands should not attempt to manage all the affairs of their households, but should "leave some things in the family to the discretion of his wife . . . and give her leave to know more than himself." Nor should husbands ever give unreasonable commands just for the sake of demonstrating their authority.[31] Authority is most effective when it is used most sparingly.

It should be laid up as one's best attire, to be worn upon high-days. A garment that comes upon a man's back every day will soon be thread-bare; so will a man's authority be worn out with over-much use.[32]

The husband who asks his wife gently rather than commanding her harshly is not only more Christlike, but is likely to get better results.

The way, then, to prevail, with least burden to the inferior, and least toil to the superior, is with mild words to wish this or that, rather than with imperious phrases to enjoin it; for most natures are much more easily persuaded than compelled. Our Saviour Christ himself doth mostly beseech his Church, though with most right he might command it. Let the husband imitate that best husband, and beware of "Do it or you had best;" and "you shall, whether you will or no;" and "I will have it so, if it be but to cross you." O no! much more comely for an husband's mouth are these words; "I pray you, let it be so; do me the kindness to do this or this."[33]

Mutual Obligations

Spirituality in Marriage

Several times in the matrimonial rite in the *Sunday Service*, reference is made to the role of spirituality in married life.[34] The concept that spirituality does play an important role was not at all foreign to Wesley's thinking. He quoted with approval William Whateley's words written many years before: ". . . that love which hath no higher aim than present wealth, peace, and happiness, deserveth no better name than a natural and a carnal love. . . Love cannot be separated from an earnest desire of [sic] the good of the party loved; and therefore spiritual love must be desirous of the spiritual good." Whateley urged married couples to pray with each other and for each other: ". . . for it is impossible that any should not love that person much and earnestly, for whom they pray much and earnestly."[35]

Wesley warned a pair of newlyweds to be careful not to become so enamored of each other that they neglected God.

> Both of you have now more need than ever continually to watch and pray, that you enter not into temptation. There will be a great danger of so cleaving to each other, as to forget God; or of being so taken up with a creature, as to abate your hunger and thirst after righteousness. There will be a danger likewise of whiling away time; of not improving it to the uttermost; of spending more of it than needs, in good sort of *talk* with each other, which yet does not quicken your souls. If you should once get into a habit of this, it will be exceeding hard to break it off.[36]

On the last day of 1767, Wesley wrote a letter in which he advised a couple to avoid frivolity, and to converse in such a way as to make them "wiser and better."

> In my last (which, it seems, you did not receive) I gave you both two advices: To beware of that levity which many serious people think innocent if not commendable between married people. Let your intimacy incite you to watch over one another that you may be uniformly and steadily serious. Do not talk on trifles with one another any more than you would with strangers; but let your freest conversations be always such as tends to make you wiser and better.[37]

In the early years of his own marriage, Wesley confessed to his wife that it had been wrong of him to laugh and trifle away time with her as he had. He expressed to her his determination that he would not fall into such a lapse again!

> I ought always to speak seriously and weightily with you, as I would with my guardian angel. Undoubtedly it is the will of God that we should be as guardian angels to each other. O what an union is that whereby we are united! The resemblance even of that between Christ

and his church. And can I laugh or trifle a moment when with you? O let that moment return no more![38]

Bishops are told in 1 Timothy 3:4 that they are to have their children "in subjection with all gravity." It was clear to Wesley why such gravity was needed: "For levity undermines all domestic authority; and this direction, by parity of reason, belongs to all parents."[39]

Nothing should be more important to parents than the spiritual nurture of their children. "The great thing we should desire of God, for our children, is, that they may *live before him*, that is, that they may be kept in covenant with him, and may have grace to walk before him *in their uprightness*."[40]

In his *Explanatory Notes upon the Old Testament*, Wesley held up Abraham as an example of a man who gave proper attention to spiritual leadership in his household.

This is a bright part of *Abraham's* character. He not only *prayed* with his family, but he *taught* them, as a man of knowledge; nay, he *commanded* them as a man in authority, and was prophet and king, as well as priest, in his own house. And he not only took care of his children, but of *his household:* his servants were *catechized servants*. Masters of families should instruct, and inspect the manners of all under their roof.[41]

The commandment regarding the Sabbath in Exodus 20:8–11 not only forbids members of the household to work on the Sabbath, but also applies the same requirement to visitors and even to the livestock! Wesley observes, "In this, as in other instances of religion, it is expected that masters of families should take care, not only to serve the Lord themselves, but that their houses also should serve him."[42]

Wesley impressed upon parents the importance of teaching their children about God. "Let our tongues be employed about the word of God, especially with our children, who must be taught this, as far more needful than the rules of decency, or the calling they are to live by." But parents should not only speak to their children about God, they should also speak to God about their children. "Parents should be particular in their addresses to God, for the several branches of their family; praying for each child, according to his particular temper, genius and disposition."[43]

Matrimonial Love

In his *Directions for Married Persons,* William Whateley taught that the love of husband and wife must be both "spiritual" and "matrimonial." "Spiritual love," according to Whateley, is the love of married persons that is based on the will and the commandment of God, not on the desirability of the spouse.

> A Christian man must love his wife not only because she is beautiful, witty, dutiful, and loving, but chiefly, because the Lord of heaven and earth hath said, "Husbands, love your wives." The wife also must love her husband, not only, or chiefly, because he is a comely man, of good means and parentage, kind to her, and of good carriage, but because he is her husband, and because God, the Sovereign of all souls, hath told women, that they ought to be lovers of their husbands. . . . If thou love they wife because she is fair, well-spoken, courteous, this is well; but what will become of thy love if all these fail, as all may, and most must fail? Thou lovest thine husband, because he is an handsome man, hath an active body, is of good wit, and of good behaviour, and useth thee well; but where shall we find thy love, if these things should alter, as all earthly things may alter? You see, then, there is no firmness in that love, which is procured only by these motives. But if thou love thy wife or husband, because God hath so bidden thee, and the Maker of all things hath enjoined it, then shalt thou find thy love constant and perpetual, as God's law continues for ever the same.[44]

The theological basis for such a "spiritual love" is the teaching in Ephesians 5:25 that husbands are to love their wives as Christ loved the church. This text, which occurs several times in the marriage service, was, for Wesley, the best description of marital love. "Here is the true model of conjugal affection. With this kind of affection, with this degree of it, and to this end, should husbands love their wives."[45]

But Whateley said that marital love must be "matrimonial" as well as "spiritual," and it is to this aspect of marital love that we now turn. "Matrimonial love" is the love of husband and wife which surpasses all other human affection.

> . . . a man must love his wife above all the creatures in the world; so must the woman her husband. Next to the living God, and our Lord Jesus Christ, the wife is to have the highest room in the husband's heart, and he in hers. No neighbour, no kinsman, no friend, no parent, no child, should be so near and dear unto the husband as his wife, nor to her as her husband.[46]

Whateley reminds his readers that the love that husband and wife are to have for each other is not based on the attractiveness of the spouse, but on the commandment of God. Therefore, the fact that a man may find another woman more attractive than his own wife should not prevent him from loving his wife above all other women.

> . . . as a man who seeeth more wit and beauty in his neighbour's son or daughter, than in his own, yea, whose own child is deformed, crooked, and dull, or untowardly and rebellious, while his neighbour's child is not only comely and quick-witted, but also gentle, dutiful, and obsequious, doth yet love his own child above his neighbour's; even so should it be betwixt husband and wife. A man may lawfully think another woman to be a better woman than his own wife, but not love the person of another more virtuous woman above the person of his own less virtuous; and so likewise may I say of the wife toward the husband.[47]

Whateley advised married persons that they could nurture their matrimonial love by regarding one another as a gift of God.

> We know, that a mean gift is much respected for the giver's sake. If men and women observe the providence of God, in bringing them together, then shall they take each other as love-tokens from God, and so shall be made very dear to each other.[48]

Economics and Domestic Management

Since eighteenth-century marriage involved economic agreements between the families, most people married within their own social class.[49] (This fact helps us better to understand Charles Wesley's concern about the impropriety of his brother's intention to marry Grace Murray.) In fact, the economic details were at times subject to public scrutiny: during the eighteenth century it was fashionable to announce the financial terms of the marriage in the local press.[50] John Wesley's own marriage was announced in this manner in the Gentleman's Magazine. "Feb. 18—Rev. Mr. John Wesley, methodist preacher,—to a merchant's widow in Threadneedle-street, with a jointure of 300 pounds per annum."[51]

Under law, a woman's children and property belonged to her husband. Because of this, some women chose to protect their property rights by living with a man, but not marrying him.[52] But in the eighteenth century, the protection of women's property rights was beginning to receive greater attention. An allowance of pocket money, known as "pin money," was often guaranteed to the wife in the marriage contract, and women were increasingly keeping more of their property under their personal control.[53] John Wesley, when he married, insisted that his wife's money should go entirely to her and to her children, not to himself.[54]

William Whateley, in the "Direction for Married Persons," argues that God does not call a man to marry without providing the means whereby he can provide adequately for his wife.[55] John Wesley once cautioned a prospective bride to consider whether her future husband would be able to support her properly.

> Is he able to keep you? I mean in such a manner as you have lived hitherto. Otherwise, remember! When poverty comes in at the door, love flies out at the window.[56]

Wesley wrote that it was the husband's duty to his wife to "provide all things needful for her and his family."[57] Whateley points out that the amount a man can spend in supporting his wife will depend, of course, on his station in life and his financial resources. But regardless of the amount of money involved, he must give to his wife "willingly, cheerfully, readily; before she asketh he must answer, and offer before she request." Husbands also have an obligation to see that their wives will be properly maintained after the husbands' death, for "the love of an husband must not die . . . with him."[58] Whateley reminds husbands that when they spoke the words of the wedding service, they gave their wives an interest in their property.

> They must have one house, and one purse; they are but one, and their estate must be one. . . . How can any man, with a good conscience, forget that part of his public and solemn covenant, wherein he endowed her with all his worldly goods?[59]

Whateley taught that married persons have duties to their families and their household in addition to their duties to each other. Among these is the obligation of parents to provide for the material needs of their children and servants.[60] Wesley recognizes that the wife shares in this responsibility when he writes of the ideal wife described in Proverbs 31, "She diligently observes the management of her domestick business, and the whole carriage of her children and servants."[61]

According to Whateley, it is the duty of husbands and wives to supervise the tasks of children and servants.[62] Whateley believed it to be vitally important that husband and wife settle any differences they may have regarding household management privately rather than in the presence of children or servants.

> If one think fit, by some little kindness, to encourage any in the family, the other must not grudge; if the one will reprove, the other must not defend; if he will correct the children, she must not grow angry and save them; neither must he save them out of her hands, when she seemeth to give chastisement. Suppose that either of them exceed in this way, in correcting either without cause or above measure, the other must not make a brawl of it before the face of the inferiors; but they must quietly debate the matter each with the other alone, and keep their disagreements of this kind from appearing in the family. For if he do, and she undo, or if she chide, and he defend, (besides the heartburnings which will grow betwixt themselves,) they shall also so lessen each other's power in the family, that both at last shall grow into contempt. . . . What one likes or dislikes let the other (at least by silence for the present) seem also to like or dislike, and let them never disagree, in admonishing, or correcting, or commending; so shall their discreet concord preserve their authority among their people, increase their love of each other, and procure amendment in their inferiors. [63]

Marital Conflict

Whateley emphasizes that married persons should seek to please one another insofar as they can without acting contrary to the will of God. Persons are not excused from this obligation because of the censoriousness of their spouse, nor are husbands permitted to apply this standard to their wives, but eschew it for themselves. For just as the wife is obligated to please her husband as an act of obedience, the husband is obligated to please his wife as an act of love.

> The scholar that hath an hard lesson, must settle more hard to his book, and not cast it away in sullenness, and say, he cannot learn it; so the husband that hath a perverse wife, or wife that hath a perverse husband, must give more diligence to give content to such husband or wife, and not carelessly cast off all, by saying, they are so cross that nothing will please them. . . . Only consider, that this point is delivered unto you amongst duties that are *mutual*. Most husbands look for it from their wives, but esteem not themselves bound to do it toward their wives: but look, what force obedience hath to tie the wife unto it, the same hath love to tie the husband. [64]

Husbands and wives should accommodate their behaviour to each other and not do things that they know will cause unnecessary aggravation. "For example; if the husband perceive the wife apt to be angry, and that such and such things will easily put her out of patience, he must pity her weakness, and carefully abstain from such things; so must she deal with him; and so must they carry themselves to each other, in regard of all other frailties, as well as anger."[65] But this commendable desire to avoid marital friction does not excuse married persons from their obligation to help a spouse overcome sins and weaknesses.

> . . . those deserve to be condemned as most treacherous to each other, who, for their own ease, will permit their yoke-fellows to sleep in sin. Let them even swear, or break the sabbath, still many yoke-fellows, for fear of a storm, can keep silence in such cases. This is to betray one another to the Devil, and to give each other leave to go to hell without check. Wouldst thou suffer thine husband to poison himself, for fear of enduring his anger if thou shouldst snatch the poison out of his hand? Wouldst thou let thy wife cut her own throat, for fear she should chafe and scold, because thou tookest the knife from her? Doubtless to let them kill each other's souls, and say nothing, for fear of passion or hard usage, is no less sinful and hurtful perfidiousness, than to give way, for quietness-sake, to their hurting of each other's bodies.[66]

But despite this obligation to assist one another in overcoming their shortcomings, married persons should be reluctant to find fault with one another.

> First then, every married couple must uphold in their hearts a good opinion of each other, so far as may possibly stand with truth. . . . Yea, for a man and wife to have in some degree an overgood opinion of each other . . . is a thing so far from blame, that it deserveth rather commendation. Certainly, then, they should be peremptorily resolved to give no credit to ungrounded, unwarranted surmises; they should by no means suffer their hearts to grow mistrustful of each other's honesty and fidelity. She must never think that he doth affect other women, unless the matter be more than manifest. She must never imagine that he doth waste or consume their estate, unless the fault be palpably and notoriously plain. He must never persuade himself that she is wanton, or given to strangers, or that she robs him, and purloins from him, unless he can make good these matters with such clearness of proof, as will not admit of any reasonable defence.[67]

Under no circumstances should one seek to humiliate one's spouse by publicly revealing that person's faults.

The publishing of each other's sins and imperfections is a monstrous treachery, and a thing than which nothing can worse become them, in the judgment of the wise. To backbite an enemy is a sin; how much more to backbite one's own yoke-fellow? . . . It is almost impossible, but that a man and wife shall sooner or later discover their weaknesses to each other; and for them to be playing the tell-tale each against the other, what soul doth not loath the thought of it?[68]

Furthermore, husbands and wives must be able to keep each other's secrets. "Wherefore, let husbands and wives always mind this: if he lay up any thing in her breast, let him find it safe there, as in a chest which cannot be opened with any pick-lock: if she commit a thing to his safe keeping, let it be safely imprisoned in his bosom; otherwise no man can help being strange towards such an one, whom experience hath convicted of blabbing."[69]

Finally, Whateley emphasizes that both husband and wife should devote their attention to fulfilling their own marital obligations, not finding fault with their partner.

. . . I must advise all Married Persons to become acquainted with these duties, and to mark their failings in the same. But mistake me not: I would that the wife should know hers, the husband his; and both, the common duties. I desire that they should observe each their own, not so much each other's failings. . . . Pass by the other's failings more easily, be more censorious towards thine own. . . . And this makes husbands and wives such ill pay-masters one to another, because they look often what is owing to them, not what they owe. . . . Every man would be a good husband, if his wife were not so bad; and she a good wife, were not he so exceedingly faulty. . . . Where you have offended, labour to see it; confess, bewail, and call for power to reform; and be not skilful to cast the fault upon another, but to cast it out of thyself. So shall your loves be sure, your hearts comfortable, your example [sic] commendable, your houses peaceful, yourselves joyful, your lives cheerful, your deaths blessed, and your memories happy for ever.[70]

Case Histories

Wesley's Sisters

Charles Wesley and his wife enjoyed a long and happy family life together, but none of John and Charles Wesley's seven sisters was so fortunate. Their sister Molly married John Whitelamb, their father's curate, in 1733, but she died in childbirth a year later. Kezzy, the youngest Wesley sister, never married and died in 1741 at the age of thirty-two.[71]

Emily, the oldest sister, was married at the age of forty-four to Robert Harper, an apothecary from Epworth. John Wesley presided at the wedding. Her husband was not able to support her, and they faced continuous financial problems; their only child died; and they drifted apart. By the end of 1738, after three years of marriage, she was constantly ill; she was forced to sell pieces of clothing to buy food; and she owed two years of back rent. When Robert died in 1740, Emily went to London to live with her brother John. From then until her death in 1771 she was completely dependent upon him for her financial support.[72]

Susanna, known affectionately as "Sukey," was the second of Wesley's sisters. Her husband, Richard Ellison, was frequently intoxicated and subjected his wife to many years of abuse and neglect. Eventually she left her husband and went to live in London, vowing never to see him again.[73]

Anne Wesley married a land surveyor named Lambert, who was also said to overindulge in alcohol. Neither Anne nor her husband was particularly religious, and the rest of the Wesley family neither saw nor heard much of her after her marriage.[74]

Hetty Wesley, her father having refused to give his consent to any of her suitors, ran away with a local lawyer named Will Atkins. The relationship lasted only one night, but it caused a serious rift between Hetty and her parents. Her father disowned her and, according to John Wesley, never spoke of her "but with the utmost detestation." Thinking herself a ruined woman, Hetty offered to marry the first respectable man who asked for her hand. She accepted the proposal of a plumber named William Wright, and although her behaviour after her marriage was "innocent," both of her parents and several of her sisters were convinced that her penitence regarding the Will Atkins affair was not genuine.[75]

In any case, her marriage was not happy. She and her husband had several children, but all but one of them died. Her husband was frequently drunk and occasionally violent. Hetty and her mother were eventually reconciled, and Hetty sometimes went to visit her. Hetty died in 1751.[76]

Patty Wesley married Westley Hall who had been one of John Wesley's students at Oxford. On a visit to Epworth with John Wesley in 1734, Hall had already met and became enamored of the youngest Wesley sister, Kezzy. Kezzy consented to Hall's proposal of marriage and they had even set a wedding date when Hall suddenly shifted his attention to Kezzy's sister Patty. Hall had been advised not to marry Kezzy by John Whitelamb, the husband of Molly Wesley. Kezzy had strongly opposed Whitelamb's marriage to her sister, and because of that, Whitelamb disliked Kezzy, although he was outwardly courteous to her. Whitelamb wrote to Hall and related a number of incidents (some of them entirely untrue, according to John Wesley) which reflected badly on Kezzy's character. Partly because of Whitelamb's interference and partly because of his own philandering spirit, Hall, abruptly and without any explanation to Kezzy, married her sister Patty. Both John and Charles Wesley believed that Hall's poor treatment of Kezzy contributed to her declining health and premature death.[77]

Hall proved to be as unpredictable in other things as he had been as a suitor. He had planned on accompanying John and Charles Wesley to Georgia and had even been ordained both deacon and priest for that very purpose, but at the last minute he decided not to go (see page 69). Theologically, Hall wandered from Methodism into Moravianism, then to Antinomianism, and finally to Deism. He was never faithful to Patty, and he both preached and practiced polygamy. He was so unrepentant about his philandering that he even brought his mistresses and illegitimate children into his own home. He and Patty had ten children together, all of whom died in infancy or childhood. Hall eventually deserted her and moved to the West Indies with one of his mistresses. Patty moved to London and lived with her sister Emily in quarters provided for them by their brother John.[78]

Westley Hall later returned to England, expressing penitence for his infidelity, and Patty forgave him. When he died in 1775, John Wesley presided at his funeral. Wesley wrote of him, "It is enough if after all his wanderings we meet again in Abraham's bosom." Patty continued to live in the place John Wesley provided for her until she died in 1791, just a few months after her brother.[79]

John and Molly Wesley

Molly Vazeille was the widow of a wealthy London merchant named Ambrose Vazeille whose estate consisted of a house on Threadneedle Street in London, a country residence in Wandsworth, and ten thousand pounds invested at 3 percent annual interest. Mr. and Mrs. Vazeille were the parents of four children.[80]

It is not known when Mrs. Vazeille first met John Wesley. We do know that Charles Wesley met her in July 1749 at the home of Edward Perronet in London. Edward was the son of Vincent Perronet, the vicar of Shoreham and a friend of the Wesleys. Vincent Perronet and Ambrose Vazeille shared a common heritage since they both came from French Huguenot families.[81] In 1750, Mrs. Vazeille accompanied Charles and Sarah Wesley on a week's visit to Sarah's parents. Upon their return to London, Mrs. Vazeille invited the Wesleys to her home on Threadneedle Street.[82]

John Wesley's journal for February 1751 reveals that Wesley sought advice from Vincent Perronet before deciding to marry Mrs. Vazeille. "Having received a full answer" from Perronet, Wesley was "clearly convinced" that he ought to proceed with his plans. But a week after deciding he would marry, Wesley slipped on the ice while hurrying across London Bridge and severely sprained his ankle. Wesley attempted to honor the preaching commitments he had made, but the pain grew worse and he was forced to spend a week letting his ankle heal. The place he chose for his convalescence was Mrs. Vazeille's house on Threadneedle Street.[83]

The following Sunday, Wesley preached in a kneeling position. The next day, February 18, Wesley had hoped to begin traveling again, but his plans had to be postponed since he still could not put any weight on his ankle. He preached again on his knees on Tuesday evening and Wednesday morning.[84]

It was sometime during these days that John Wesley was married. Wesley himself made no mention of his wedding in his journal.[85] For the date of his marriage, we are dependent on two published accounts, one of which gives the date as 18 February and the other as 19 February 1751. The presiding minister is believed to have been the Reverend Charles Manning, a mutual friend of the bride and the groom.[86] The statement in the *Bristol Weekly Intelligencer* of 2 March 1751 that Charles Wesley presided at his brother's wedding is highly dubious, since, as we shall see, Charles strongly disapproved of John's marriage.[87] John Wesley was forty-seven years old at the time of his marriage; his bride was forty-one.[88]

Since Wesley was still not able to put any weight on his ankle, one can only wonder what the wedding must have looked like. Did Wesley sit through the entire ceremony, was he married on his knees, or did he stand next to his bride balancing himself on one foot? In any event, it must have been a peculiar sight.

The situation was further complicated by Charles Wesley's reaction to his brother's wedding plans. Although the brothers had agreed not to marry without the other's consent, John remembered what had happened sixteen months previously when he told Charles that he wanted to marry Grace Murray. This time John *told* rather than *asked* his brother about his intentions, and he did not even tell him who the bride was to be! Charles described his reaction in his journal.

> Sat., February 2d. My brother, returned from Oxford, sent for and told me *he was resolved to marry!* I was thunderstruck, and could only answer, he had given me the first blow, and his marriage would come like the *coup de grace*. Trusty Ned Perronet followed, and told me, the person was Mrs. Vazeille! one of whom I had never had the least suspicion. I refused his company to the chapel, and retired to mourn with my faithful Sally. I groaned all the day, and several following ones, under my own and the people's burden. I could eat no pleasant food, nor preach, nor rest, either by night or by day.[89]

Charles recorded in his journal for Sunday, 17 February that his listened to his brother's public explanation of his decision to marry.

> At the Foundery heard my brother's lamentable apology, which made us all hide our faces. Several days afterwards I was one of the last that heard of his unhappy marriage.[90]

The following Sunday, Ebenezer Blackwell, a friend of both the Wesley brothers and Mrs. Vazeille, sought to bring about a reconciliation. Charles recorded, "After sacrament Mr. Blackwell fell upon me in a manner peculiar to himself, brating, [*sic*] driving, dragging me to my sister."[91] A few days later, John Wesley and his wife paid Charles a cordial visit.

> My brother came to the chapel house with his wife. I was glad to see him; saluted her; stayed to hear him preach; but ran away when he began his apology.[92]

By the middle of March, Charles was ready to make peace with his brother and his new sister-in-law.

> *Thur. 14.*—Saw the necessity of reconciliation with my brother, and resolved to save the trouble of umpires.
> *Fri. 15.*—Called on my sister, kissed and assured her I was perfectly reconciled to her and to my brother. . . .
> *Tues. 19.*—Brought my wife and sister together, and took all opportunities of showing the latter my sincere respect and love. . . .

Fri. 22.—With my brother; said I desired entire reconciliation, that all the advantage Satan had gained was through our want of mutual confidence; that I did not believe him in as dangerous situation as he was before his marriage.[93]

On 4 March, two weeks after his wedding, "being tolerably able to ride, though not to walk," John Wesley set out for Bristol. He returned to London on 21 March, but left again on 27 March.[94] Before the day was over, he wrote an affectionate letter to his wife.

My dear Molly,
    Do I write too soon? Have you not above all the people in the world a right to hear from me as soon as possibly I can? You have surely a right to every proof of love I can give, and to all the little help which is in my power. For you have given me even your own self. Oh, how can we praise God enough for making us helps meet for each other! I am utterly astonished at His goodness. Let not only our lips but our lives show forth His praise![95]

He closed his letter with the direction, "If any letter comes to you directed to the Rev. John Wesley, open it; it is for yourself."[96] As we will see, this was a permission he would later regret and would attempt to retract.

Molly attempted to travel with her husband, but the wealthy London widow was not well suited for the rigors of an itinerant life. Though John Wesley spoke with optimism in a letter to their friend Ebenezer Blackwell, his own words betray the fact that Molly had not been enjoying her travels.

After taking a round of between three and four hundred miles, we came hither yesterday in the afternoon. My wife is at least as well as when we left London: The more she travels, the better she bears it. It gives us yet another proof, that whatever God calls us to, he will fit us for; so that we have no need to take thought for the morrow. Let the morrow take thought for the things of itself. I was at first a little afraid she would not so well understand the behaviour of a Yorkshire mob; but there has been no trial: Even the Methodists are now at peace throughout the kingdom.[97]

This letter should be contrasted with another which Wesley wrote to Blackwell after Molly had decided not to travel with her husband any longer.

In my last journey into the north, all my patience was put to the proof again and again; and all my endeavour to please, yet without success. In my present journey I leap as broke from chains. I am content with whatever entertainment I meet with, and my companions are always in good humour, "because they are with me." This must be the spirit of all who take journeys with me. If a dinner ill dressed, a hard bed, a poor room, a shower of rain, or a dirty road, will put them out of humour, it lays a burden upon me, greater than all the rest put together. By the grace of God, I never fret. I repine at nothing: I am discontented with nothing. And to have persons at my ear, fretting and murmuring at everything, is like tearing the flesh off my bones.[98]

It was in September 1755 that Molly first accused her husband of infidelity. Wesley explained to Ebenezer Blackwell how this came about.

Charles Perronet being out of town last Saturday, my packet, directed to him, fell into other hands. This has raised a violent storm; for it contained a few lines which I writ to Mrs. Lefevre, in answer to a letter she sent me the week before concerning Mr. Furly. It is pity! I should be glad if I had to do with reasonable people.[99]

Many years later, Wesley recounted this episode in a letter to his wife.

In the midst of this you drew new matter of offence from my acquaintance with Mrs. Lefevre, a dove-like woman, full of faith and humble love and harmless as a little child. I should have rejoiced to converse with her frequently and largely; but for *your* sake I abstained. I did not often talk with her at all, and visited her but twice or thrice in two years. Notwithstanding which, though you sometimes said you thought her a good woman, yet at other times you did not scruple to say you "questioned if I did not lie with her." And afterward you seemed to make no question of it.[100]

Later, it was Sarah Ryan, the housekeeper at Kingswood, who was the object of Mrs. Wesley's jealousy (see pages 23–24). Molly objected to the affectionate letters that her husband wrote to the housekeeper. Although Wesley no longer wanted his wife to open his correspondence, Molly continued to open and read her husband's mail. But on one particular occasion, Molly's snooping actually brought about a temporary reconciliation between the Wesleys. John Wesley described what happened in his next letter to Sarah Ryan.

Last Friday, after many severe words, my wife left me, vowing she would see me no more. As I had wrote to you the same morning, I began to reason with myself, till I almost doubted whether I had done well in writing, or whether I ought to write to you at all. After prayer that doubt was taken away. Yet I was almost sorry that I had written that morning. In the evening, while I was preaching at the chapel, she came into the chamber where I had left my clothes, searched my pockets, and found the letter there, which I had finished, but had not sealed. While she read it, God broke her heart; and I afterwards found her in such a temper as I have not seen her in for several years. She has continued in the same ever since.[101]

But a few weeks later, Wesley was again complaining of how tiring it was "being continually watched over for evil, the having every word I spoke, every action I did, small and great, watched over with no friendly eye."[102] Later in the month, Wesley attempted to negotiate a truce with his wife, but once again, an apparent breakthrough ended in frustration.

Sunday, February 25, 1758, you went into my study, opened my bureau, and took many of my letters and papers. But on your restoring most of them two days after, I said, "Now, my dear, let all that is past be forgotten; and if either of us find any fresh ground of complaint, let us tell it to Mr. Blackwell, or Jo. Jones, or Tho. Walsh, but to no other person whatever." You agreed; and on Monday, March 6, when I took my leave of you to set out for Ireland, I thought we had as tender a parting as we had had for several years.

To confirm this good understanding, I wrote to you a few days after all that was in my heart. But from your answer I learned it had a quite contrary effect: you *resented* it deeply; so that for ten or twelve weeks together, though I wrote letter after letter, I received not one line. Meantime you told Mrs. Vigor and twenty more, "Mr. Wesley *never* writes to *me*. You must inquire concerning him of Sarah Ryan; he writes to her *every* week." So far from it, that I did not write to her at all for above twelve weeks before I left Ireland. Yet I really thought you would not tell a willful lie—at least, not in cold blood; till poor, dying T. Walsh asked me at Limerick, "How did you apart with Mrs. W. last time?" On my saying, "Very affectionately," he replied, "Why, what a woman is this! She told me your parting words were, 'I hope to see your wicked face no more.'"[103]

On 18 December 1758, for the first time, Wesley set out on a trip without telling his wife where he was going.[104] Five days later, Wesley wrote to his wife an angry letter in which he strongly asserted his right to choose his own company

I was much concerned, the night before I left London, at your unkind and unjust accusation. You accused *me* of unkindness, cruelty, and what not. And why so? Because I insist on choosing my own company! because I insist upon conversing, by speaking or writing, with those whom I (not you) judge proper! For more than seven years this has been a bone of contention between you and and me. And it is so still. For I will not, I cannot, I dare not give it up. But then *you* will rage and fret and call me names. I am sorry for it. But I cannot help it. I still do and must insist that I have a right to choose my own company.[105]

On 23 October 1759, Wesley wrote a letter to Molly in which he identified ten specific items that he disliked about her.

I dislike (1) Your showing any one my letters and private papers without my leave. . . .

I dislike (2) Not having the command of my own house, not being at liberty to invite even my nearest relations so much as to drink a dish of tea without disobliging *you*. I dislike (3) The being myself a prisoner in my own house; the having my chamber door watched continually so that no person can go in or out but such as have your good leave. I dislike (4) The being but a prisoner at large, even when I go abroad, inasmuch as you are highly disgusted if I do not give you an account of every place I go to and every person with whom I converse. I dislike (5) The not being safe in my own house. My house is *not* my castle. I cannot call even my study, even my bureau, my own. They are liable to be plundered every day. . . . I dislike (6) Your treatment of my servants. . .

I dislike (7) Your talking against me behind my back, and that every day and almost every hour of the day; making my faults (real or supposed) the standing topic of your conversation. I dislike (8) Your slandering me, laying to my charge things which you know are false. . . . I dislike (9) Your common custom of saying things that are not true. . . . I dislike (10) Your extreme, immeasurable bitterness to all who endeavour to defend my character (as my brother, Joseph Jones, Clayton Carthy), breaking out even into foul, unmannerly language, such as ought not to defile a gentlewoman's lips if she did not believe one word of the Bible.[106]

In another letter, Wesley tried to convince Molly that it was her duty to obey him.

Alas, that to this hour you should neither know your duty nor be willing to learn it! Indeed, if you was a wise, whether a good woman or not, you would long since have given me a carte blanche: you would have said, "Tell me what to do, and I will do it; tell me what to avoid, and I will avoid it. I promised to obey you, and I will keep my word. Bid me to do anything, everything. In whatever is not sinful, I obey. You direct, I will follow the direction."

. . . . This must be your indispensable duty, till (1) I am an adulterer; (2) you can prove it. . . . Consequently, every act of disobedience is an act of rebellion against God and the King. . .[107]

Despite all that had transpired, for the next few years the marriage of John and Molly Wesley was relatively tranquil. In 1763 Wesley wrote to his brother Charles regarding his wife, "She is quite peaceable and loving to all." And in 1766 he wrote to Charles, "My wife continues in an amazing temper. Miracles are not ceased. Not one jarring sting. O let us live now!"[108]

But unfortunately, such domestic bliss did not continue. Molly Wesley left her husband again in 1767 but returned in 1768, left in 1769 and returned in 1770, left in 1771 and returned in 1772.[109] After one of those departures, Wesley wrote in his journal, "For what cause I know not, my wife set out for Newcastle, purposing never to return. *Non eam reliqui; non dimisi; non revocabo.*"[110]

Molly Wesley left her husband for the last time in 1774 and never returned. John Wesley wrote her a letter that year in which he defended his own conduct, repeated his complaints about her, and expressed hope that they could still work things out!

As yet the breach may be repaired; you have wronged me much, but not beyond forgiveness. I love you still, and am as clear from all other women as the day I was born.[111]

The Wesleys came close to another reconciliation in 1777. Molly seemed willing to return, but John insisted upon certain conditions.

I sincerely wish a reunion with you if it could be upon Good terms. Otherwise it would not continue: And then the last error would be worse than the first. But what are those terms on which it probably would continue? . . .

. . . . A few days since I met you (to my great surprize) you seemed willing to return. I was willing to receive you upon these terms, 1. Restore my Papers. 2. Promise to take no more.

But upon reflection I see I was too hasty. For you have given Copies of my Papers, and those you cannot recall. Likewise you have spoken all manner of evil against me, particularly to my Enemies, and the Enemies of the Cause I live to support. . . .

Things standing thus, if I was to receive you just now, without any Acknowledgment or reparation of these wrongs, it would be esteemed by all reasonable men, a Confirmation of all you have said. . . .

All you can do now, if you are ever so willing, is to Unsay what you have said. For instance: You have said over and over that I have lived in Adultery these twenty years. Do you believe this or do you not? If you do, how can you think of living with such a Monster? If you do not, give it to me under your hand? Is not this the least that you can do?[112]

On 2 October 1778, Wesley wrote a final letter to Molly.

As it is doubtful, considering your age and mine, whether we may meet any more in the world, I think it right to tell you my mind once for all without either anger or bitterness. . . . You have published my (real or supposed) faults, not to one or two intimates only (though perhaps that would have been too much), but to all Bristol, to all London, to all England, to all Ireland. Yea, you did whatever in you lay to publish to all the world, thereby designing to put a sword into my enemies' hands. . . . If you were to live a thousand years, you could not undo the mischief you have done. And till you have done all you can towards it, I bid you farewell.[113]

In August 1779, Molly's son-in-law, a leader of the Methodist society at Newcastle named William Smith, attempted to work out a reconciliation between his mother-in-law and her husband, but to no avail:

I talked freely to both parties, and did all in my power to lay a foundation for future union; but alas! all my attempts proved unsuccessful. I had to leave matters not better than I found them.[114]

Molly died on 8 October 1781. Wesley, as usual, was traveling, and did not learn of his wife's death until four days later:

I came to London, and was informed that my wife died on Monday. This evening she was buried, though I was not informed of it till a day or two after.[115]

Rarely does the blame for a failed marriage rest entirely with only one of the partners, and the marriage of John and Molly Wesley was no exception. But Wesley's biographers, though not entirely exonerating Wesley of any blame, are usually sharply critical of Molly. Luke Tyerman, for example, referred to Molly as "his twitting wife" and said, "In no way was she a helpmeet for him. As a rule, she was a bitter, unmitigated curse."[116] Robert Southey, in his biography of Wesley, grouped Molly with Xanthippe and Job's wife as "the three outstanding examples of the world's bad women." Both Nehemiah Curnock (who edited an edition of Wesley's journal) and John Telford speak of her mental instability. The tendency of Wesley's biographers to idolize John and vilify Molly was aptly described by Samuel Rogal when he wrote, "Certain Wesleyan scholars of the late nineteenth and early twentieth centuries determined to promote the role of Molly Vazeille as a dark shadow across the otherwise angelic path trod by the Pauline image of her second husband."[117]

In recent years, however, commentators have taken a more balanced view of John Wesley's marriage and have noted that, although Molly could be difficult at times, so could John. Kenneth Collins, in his analysis of John Wesley's marriage, lists four ways in which Wesley contributed to the marriage's failure, beginning with Wesley's high regard for celibacy as the preferred state of life for a Christian. Marriage was far less important to Wesley than was his sense of a divine calling to his ministry. Secondly, "a person so driven in the pursuit of ministry, like Wesley, so punctilious in his use and valuation of time, could only appear as unkind, cold, and neglectful to the suffering (and at times sick) spouse." Third, Wesley failed to recognize that some of Molly's conduct, such as her displays of jealousy and her theft of his letters, was a response to her feelings of being neglected. By focusing on Molly's conduct, Wesley was able to avoid dealing with the underlying issues in their relationship. Finally, Wesley's authoritarian style and his demand for obedience combined with the self-righteous way in which he enumerated his wife's faults while neglecting his own all contributed to the failure of his marriage.[118]

The contrast between the ideal family life described by William Whateley and Wesley's personal experience is striking. How can we account for this discrepancy? It is important to remember that for Whateley as well as for Wesley, Christian marriage should further the spiritual growth of the partners. John Wesley took this responsibility so seriously that he had actually apologized to his wife for laughing with her and not always speaking "seriously and weightily" with her (pages 106–7). Furthermore, who could deny the importance of Wesley's work among the Methodist societies? Was it not unreasonable of Molly to object to her husband's travels and frequent absences from home when he was so clearly doing the work of God? Whateley also taught that husbands were to correct their wives. This was consistent with Wesley's penchant for relating to women as a spiritual guide or mentor. He therefore understood it as his conjugal duty to correct his wife for her faulty sense of priorities. Although Whateley's understanding of married life was essentially positive, Wesley's application of Whateley's principles to his own situation only made matters worse.

One naturally wonders how different Wesley's personal life might have been had he married Grace Murray instead of Molly Vazeille. Certainly Grace did not object to traveling with him, and she was an active leader in the Methodist societies, unlike Molly, who was only conventionally religious at best. But Grace Murray also displayed some jealousy during her romance with John Wesley. Would her response have been that much different from Molly's to her husband's warmly affectionate relationship with a number of other women? Augustin Leger, the author of the most thorough study yet published of Wesley's relationship with Grace Murray, was skeptical that Wesley and Grace would have been happy together. Leger said, "Without any particular dispensation of Providence, his wedding at all was naturally bound to prove a failure; and the odds are that the event would have been very nearly the same had he married Grace Murray."[119]

When Wesley died in 1791, an obituary in the *Gentleman's Magazine* reflected the controversy surrounding his marriage.

> . . . he married a lady, from whom he afterward parted, and she died in 1781; by her he had no children. This separation, from whatever motives it originated, we have heard some of his followers say, was the only blot on his character. Others have observed on this head, that nothing could be more effectually disappointed than ambition or avarice in an union with John Wesley.[120]

But perhaps the most trenchant comment on his marriage came from Wesley himself. In a letter written less than a year before his death, Wesley recommended celibacy to all who could continue in that state, and then observed regarding his own life, "I married because I needed a home in order to recover my health; and I did recover it. But I did not seek happiness thereby, and I did not find it."[121]

Conclusions

We began this study with the questions, "Why did Wesley make the changes that he did in the marriage service from the Book of Common Prayer? Why did he delete the words he deleted and retain the words he retained?" We are now in a position to summarize our findings.

If we look to Wesley for guidance that can be applied directly to contemporary matrimonial rites, we will be disappointed. Only a few general principles gleaned from Wesley's practice can be transferred to the current context.

For instance, Wesley's willingness to jettison certain outmoded traditions is instructive. Stevenson notes that no service in the prayer book has changed as little over the centuries as the service of matrimony.[1] Wesley, however, was able to adapt an existing liturgy to fit a changing social context. At a time when family life is changing as much as it is today, we are in sore need of the wisdom and skill required to revise liturgical texts so that they more adequately address the contemporary context.

We should also note Wesley's preference for hymn singing rather than music performed by a soloist or an ensemble. For Wesley, worship was an activity of the entire congregation, not a performance staged for spectators. Wedding congregations usually do not actively participate in the liturgy; Wesley's example points out the inadequacy of this practice.

But aside from these general observations, we do not find in Wesley's matrimonial rite ideas or practices that ought to be revived in weddings today. This is partly because of the great difference in social customs between Wesley's day and our own, but it is also because of John Wesley's beliefs about the nature of marriage. It would be surprising if someone who devalued marriage in the way that Wesley did were to create a marriage liturgy that served as a model for matrimonial rites centuries later.

Wesley's attitude toward marriage was largely a result of his Anglican heritage which, unlike the Puritan tradition, always retained a certain ambivalence in its attitude toward marriage, particularly the marriage of clergy. Although the Roman teaching that celibacy was required of clergy and those in religious orders was officially repudiated, there still was considerable resistance to the marriage of clergy. This ambivalence is reflected in the prayer book liturgy, which teaches that marriage was ordained primarily as a means of procreation and secondarily as a remedy for fornication. Its value as a source of help and companionship for the marriage partners themselves is less important in Anglican thought than are the first two purposes mentioned. This results in an understanding of marriage which views it as a necessity of human society, but not as a way of life that is to be desired.

This is the understanding of marriage which John Wesley was taught by the prescribed liturgy of his church. For Wesley, the ultimate liturgical standards were the scriptures and the practices of the early church. But since there was no ancient Christian marriage rite to which Wesley could look as a model, the prayer book service became his most authoritative liturgical source.

In the *Sunday Service,* Wesley retained the prayer book's ordering of the purposes for which marriage was ordained. Although this suggests that for Wesley, procreation was the primary purpose of marriage, Wesley's other writings point to a different conclusion. For Wesley says little about procreation, but a great deal about the advantages of celibacy. Clearly, it is the *second* traditional purpose of marriage which figures most prominently in his thinking. For those who are not able to remain continent, marriage is the answer. In addition, were procreation the most important reason for marriage, it would be difficult to explain Wesley's decision to marry a widow in her forties who already had several children.

There was a time when stressing procreation as the chief purpose of marriage made sense. John Wesley's mother, for instance, gave birth to nineteen children, but only ten survived to adulthood. There was incentive to produce a large number of children in the eighteenth century because of the infant mortality rate, a life expectancy that was considerably shorter than it is in developed countries today, and the necessity of large families to help with the many tasks required for economic survival. But today our problem is overpopulation, not a population shortage. Because of our increased life expectancy, many couples will live together for decades after their children leave home. If the chief purpose of marriage is procreation, does that not imply that the later years of a long-standing marriage are less valuable? What of couples who marry later in life, or those unable to have children, or those who have undergone voluntary sterilization because they have already had several children with a previous spouse? As the Puritans sarcastically pointed out, if procreation were the chief purpose of marriage, then polygamy was certainly a more effective means of accomplishing the goal than monogamy (page 54). The Puritan objections to the Anglican ordering of the purposes of marriage are, if anything, even more relevant today.

Why was Wesley's marriage as unhappy as it was? Much has been written about Molly's intense jealousy, although there is another factor that is at least as important, and that is Wesley's commitment to itinerancy. After Charles Wesley married, he traveled less and less.[2] For John, such a slackening of the pace was unthinkable. Molly made an effort to travel with him at first, but it was a life to which she was not well suited. This divergence in lifestyles made the building of a satisfying family life extremely difficult.

Wesley recognized the threat that marriage posed to an itinerant ministry, and he constantly urged his preachers to avoid marriage whenever possible. Wesley's position was reiterated in American Methodism by Francis Asbury. When Asbury discovered at the 1809 Virginia Methodist Annual Conference that only three of the eighty-four preachers in the conference were married, he regarded that as good news, as revealed by his journal entry for that day:

> The high taste of these southern folks will not permit their families to be degraded by an alliance with a Methodist travelling preacher; and thus, involuntary celibacy is imposed upon us: all the better; anxiety about worldly possessions does not stop our course.[3]

When Asbury was told that a particular preacher was going to be married, he lamented, "I believe the devil and women will get all my preachers."[4] He knew that married preachers were likely to drop out of the itinerancy.

Over the next few decades, the number of married clergy increased, much to the dismay of the bishops who expressed their concern in the episcopal address at the 1844 Methodist General Conference.

> The admission of married men into the itineracy had a debilitating influence upon the energies of the itinerant system. . . . A large proportion of the young preachers marry before they graduate to the Eldership, and no small number while they are on trial. And this has

almost ceased to be an objection to their trial. In general, it is quite sufficient that they have *"married prudently."*

It is not easy to calculate the extent of the influence of this practice to enervate the operations of the itinerant ministry. . . . The circuits which would have received and sustained them with cordiality as single men, in consideration of their youth and want of experience, have very different views and feelings when they are sent to them with the encumbrance of a family. . .

It is to be feared that these men have either mistaken their calling in the beginning, or by early temptation lost the spirit and power of it.[5]

But the tension between marriage and itinerancy continued, and has not yet been resolved. Today many spouses of clergy have their own careers and are reluctant to move whenever and wherever the bishop might decide. Clergy couples pose special challenges and opportunities for the itinerant system. Divorced clergy may need to stay within commuting distance of children who are living with a former spouse. An itinerant ministry can work well when most of the preachers are single, as they were in the early years of Methodism, both in England and in America. But those days are gone and are unlikely to return. The traditional system of deploying Methodist clergy must continue to evolve in light of the current realities.

For Wesley, marriage carried with it the danger of idolatry: loving a human being more than one loves God. God, for Wesley, was the great rival, whose service must always supersede every other concern. Wesley was a firm believer in a disciplined spiritual life; it was in fact because of his systematic observance of pious practices that he and his colleagues were nicknamed "Methodists." That is why Wesley told his wife it had been wrong for them to "trifle away time." Everything they did should be directed toward the goal of increasing their love and devotion to God. To many people (including Charles Wesley) spending time at home with one's wife and family is intrinsically worthwhile; to John Wesley, it was a distraction from his ministry.

Nowhere is Wesley's understanding of family life as a distraction from divine service revealed more blatantly and shockingly than in the letter he wrote to his sister Patty following the loss of three children, all of whom died in infancy:

I believe the death of your children is a great instance of the goodness of God toward you. You have often mentioned to me how much of your time they took up. Now that time is restored to you, and you have nothing to do but to serve the Lord without carefulness and without distraction, till you are sanctified in body, soul, and spirit.[6]

Frederick Maser commented in regard to this letter, "It is doubtful if, from the beginning of time, any pastor except John Wesley, would have tried to comfort a mother by assuring her that the loss of her children is a 'great instance of the goodness of God.'"[7] As Pamela Couture has observed, "Evidently, John failed to notice that in spending time caring for her children, she was also 'serving the Lord.'"[8]

There are few women who could be happy with a husband who took such an attitude; Molly Wesley was apparently not among them. Why John and Molly Wesley married each other is not clear; our sources for this information are rather meager. We know much more about John Wesley's courtship of Grace Murray.

Grace may in fact have been the only woman, other than his mother, with whom John Wesley enjoyed genuine emotional intimacy and a true sense of partnership. Wesley saw in her someone who could be his partner in the work of God, not a rival who would draw him away. But when she married John Bennet, a devastated and despairing John Wesley concluded that even the most promising and certain of earthly loves are frail, unreliable phantoms that might vanish in an instant. This perspective was to color his thinking for the rest of his days. Thrown back upon the one source of love that he knew would never end, Wesley poured out his broken heart to God in some of the most eloquent and passionate poetry ever to come forth from his pen.

> Teach me, from every pleasing Snare
> To keep the Issues of my Heart:
> Be thou my Love, my Joy, my Fear!
> Thou my eternal Portion art.
> Be thou my never-failing Friend
> And love, O love me to the End![9]

Appendix A:
The Form of Solemnization of Matrimony in the Book of Common Prayer and the *Sunday Service*

Book of Common Prayer (1662)
The Form of Solemnization of
MATRIMONY.
*First the Banns of all that
are to be married together,
must be published in the
Church three several Sundays
or Holy-days, in the time of
Divine Service, immediately
before the Sentences for the
Offertory; the Curate saying
after the accustomed Manner,*
I Publish the Banns of
Marriage between M. of _____
and N. of _____. If any of you
know cause or just
impediment, why these two
persons should not be joined
together in holy Matrimony,
ye are to declare it: This
is the first (*second* or
third) time of asking.
*And if the Persons that are
to be married dwell in divers
Parishes, the Banns must be
asked in both Parishes; and
the Curate of the one Parish
shall not solemnize Matrimony
betwixt them, without a
Certificate of the Banns being
thrice asked from the Curate
of the Other Parish.*

The Sunday Service (1784)
The Form of Solemnization of
MATRIMONY.
*First, the Banns of all that
are to be married together,
must be published in the
Congregation, three several
Sundays, in the Time of
Divine Service; the Minister
saying after the accustomed
Manner,*
I Publish the Banns of
Marriage between M. of _____
and N. of _____. If any of
you know cause or just
impediment, why these two
persons should not be joined
together in holy Matrimony,
ye are to declare it: This
is the first (*second,* or
third) time of asking.

*At the day and time appointed
for solemnization of
Matrimony, the Persons to be
married shall come into the
Body of the Church with their
friends and neighbours: And
there standing together, the
Man on the right hand, and
the Woman on the left, the
Priest shall say,*
Dearly beloved, we are
gathered together here in
the sight of God, and in the
face of this Congregation, to
join together this Man and
this Woman in holy Matrimony;
which is an honourable
Estate, instituted of God in
the time of mans innocency,
signifying unto us the
mystical union that is
betwixt Christ and his
Church: which holy estate
Christ adorned and beautified
with his presence, and first
miracle that he wrought in
Cana of Galilee; and is
commended of Saint Paul to be
honourable among all men; and
therefore is not by any to be
enterprised, nor taken in
hand unadvisedly, lightly or
wantonly, to satisfy mens
carnal lusts and appetites,
like brute beasts that have
no understanding; but
reverently, discreetly,
advisedly, soberly, and in
the fear of God; duly
considering the causes for
which Matrimony was ordained:
First, it was ordained for
the procreation of children,
to be brought up in the fear
and nurture of the Lord, and
to the praise of his holy

*At the Day and Time appointed
for Solemnization of
Matrimony, the Persons to be
married, standing together,
the Man on the Right Hand,
and the Woman on the Left,
the Minister shall say,*
Dearly beloved, we are
gathered together here in
the sight of God, and in the
face of this Congregation,
to join together this Man
and this Woman in holy
Matrimony; which is an
honourable estate, instituted
of God in the time of man's
innocency, signifying unto us
the mystical union that is
betwixt Christ and his
Church: which holy estate
Christ adorned and beautified
with his presence, and first
miracle that he wrought in
Cana of Galilee; and is
commended of St. Paul to be
honourable among all men; and
therefore is not by any to be
enterprized, or taken in
hand unadvisedly, lightly, or
wantonly, to satisfy men's
carnal lusts and appetites,
like brute beasts, that have
no understanding; but
reverently, discreetly,
advisedly, soberly, and in
the fear of God; duly
considering the causes for
which Matrimony was ordained.
First, It was ordained for
the procreation of children,
to be brought up in the fear
and nurture of the Lord, and
to the praise of his holy

Name.

Secondly, it was ordained
for a remedy against sin, and
to avoid fornication; that
such persons as have not the
gift of continency, might
marry, and keep themselves
undefiled members of Christs
body.

Thirdly, it was ordained
for the mutual society, help,
and comfort that the one
ought to have of the other,
both in prosperity and
adversity: Into which holy
estate these two persons
present come now to be
joined. Therefore if any man
can shew any just cause why
they may not lawfully be
joined together, let him now
speak, or else hereafter for
ever hold his peace.

And also speaking to the
Persons that shall be
married, he shall say,
I Require and charge you
both (as ye will answer at
the dreadful day of judgment,
when the secrets of all
hearts shall be disclosed)
that if either of you know
any impediment, why ye may
not be lawfully joined
together in Matrimony, ye do
now confess it. For be ye
well assured, that so many as
are coupled together
otherwise than Gods Word doth
allow, are not joined
together by God, neither is
their Matrimony lawful.
At which day of Marriage,
if any man do alledge and
declare any impediment why

Name.

Secondly, It was ordained
for a remedy against sin, and
to avoid fornication; that
such persons as have not the
gift of continency, might
marry, and keep themselves
undefiled members of Christ's
body.
Thirdly, It was ordained
for the mutual society, help,
and comfort, that the one
ought to have of the other,
both in prosperity and
adversity.

Into which holy estate
these two persons present
come now to be joined.
Therefore if any man can
shew any just cause why they
may not lawfully be joined
together, let him now speak,
or else hereafter for ever
hold his peace.
And also speaking unto the
Persons that are to be
married, he shall say,
I Require and charge you
both (as you will answer at
the dreadful day of judgment,
when the secrets of all
hearts shall be disclosed)
that if either of you know
any impediment why you may
not be lawfully joined
together in Matrimony, you do
now confess it. For be ye
well assured, that so many as
are coupled together
otherwise than God's Word
doth allow, are not joined
together by God, neither is
their Matrimony lawful.

*they may not be coupled together
in Matrimony by Gods Law,
or the Laws of this Realm;
and will be bound, and sufficient
Sureties with him, to the
Parties, or else put in a
Caution (to the full value
of such charges as the Persons
to be married do thereby sustain)
to prove his Allegation; then
the Solemnization must be
deferred, until such time
as the truth be tried.
If no impediment be alledged,
then shall the Curate say
unto the Man,*
N. Wilt thou have this Woman
to thy wedded Wife, to live
together after Gods
ordinance, in the holy estate
of Matrimony? Wilt thou love
her, comfort her, honour and
keep her in sickness and in
health; and forsaking all
other, keep thee only unto
her, so long as ye both shall
live?
*The Man shall answer, I will.
Then shall the Priest say
unto the Woman,*
N. Wilt thou have this Man to
thy wedded Husband, to live
together after Gods
ordinance, in the holy estate
of Matrimony? Wilt thou obey
him, serve him, love, honour,
and keep him in sickness and
in heath; and forsaking all
other, keep thee only unto
him, so long as ye both shall
live?
*The Woman shall answer,
I will.
Then shall the Minister say,*
Who giveth this Woman to be
married to this Man?
Then shall they give their

*If no Impediment be alledged,
then shall the Minister say
unto the Man,*
M. Wilt thou have this woman
to thy wedded wife, to live
together after God's
ordinance, in the holy estate
of Matrimony? Wilt thou love
her, comfort her, honour, and
keep her, in sickness, and in
health; and forsaking all
other, keep thee only unto
her, so long as you both
shall live?
*The Man shall answer, I will.
Then shall the Minister say
unto the Woman,*
N. Wilt thou have this Man to
thy wedded Husband, to live
together after God's
ordinance, in the holy estate
of Matrimony? Wilt thou obey
him, serve him, love, honour,
and keep him, in sickness and
in heath; and forsaking all
other, keep thee only unto
him, so long as you both
shall live?
The Woman shall answer,
I will.

troth to each other in this
manner.
The Minister receiving the
Woman at her Fathers or
Friends hands, shall cause
the Man with his right hand
to take the Woman by her
right hand, and to say after
him, as followeth:
I N. take thee N. to my
wedded Wife, to have and to
hold from this day forward,
for better for worse, for
richer for poorer, in
sickness and in health, to
love and to cherish, till
death us do part, according
to Gods holy ordinance; and
thereto I plight thee my
troth.
Then shall they loose their
hands, and the woman with her
right hand taking the Man by
his right hand, shall
likewise say after the
Minister:
I N. take thee N. to my
wedded Husband, to have and
to hold from this day
forward, for better for
worse, for richer for poorer,
in sickness and in health, to
love, cherish, and to obey,
till death us do part,
according to Gods holy
ordinance; and thereto I
give thee my troth.
Then shall they again loose
their hands, and the Man shall
give unto the Woman a Ring,
laying the same upon the Book,
with the accustomed duty to
the Priest and Clerk. And
the Priest taking the Ring,
shall deliver it unto the
Man, to put it upon the fourth
finger of the Womans left

Then the Minister shall cause
the Man with his Right Hand
to take the woman by her
Right Hand, and to say after
him as followeth:

I M. take thee N. to be my
wedded wife, to have and to
hold, from this day forward,
for better for worse, for
richer for poorer, in
sickness and in health, to
love and to cherish, till
death us do part, according
to God's holy ordinance; and
thereto I plight thee my
Faith.
Then shall they loose their
Hands, and the Woman with her
Right Hand taking the Man by
his Right Hand, shall
likewise say after the
Minister:
I N. take thee M. to be my
wedded Husband, to have and
to hold, from this day
forward, for better for
worse, for richer for poorer,
in sickness and in health, to
love, cherish, and to obey,
till death us do part,
according to God's holy
ordinance; and thereto I
give thee my Faith.

hand. And the Man holding
the Ring there, and taught
by the Priest, shall say,
With this Ring I thee wed,
with my body I thee worship,
and with all my worldly goods
I thee endow: In the Name
of the Father, and of the
Son, and of the Holy Ghost.
Amen.
Then the Man leaving the Ring
upon the fourth finger of
the Womans left hand, they
shall both kneel down, and
the Minister shall say,
Let us pray.
O Eternal God, Creator and
Preserver of all mankind,
giver of all spiritual grace,
the author of everlasting
life; Send thy blessing upon
these thy servants, this Man
and this Woman, whom we bless
in thy Name; that as Isaac
and Rebecca lived faithfully
together, so these persons
may surely perform and keep
the vow and covenant betwixt
them made (whereof this Ring
given and received is a token
and pledge) and may ever
remain in perfect love and
peace together, and live
according to thy laws,
through Jesus Christ our
Lord. *Amen.*
Then shall the Priest join
their right hands together,
and say,
Those whom God hath joined
together, let no man put
asunder.
Then shall the Minister speak
unto the People:
Forasmuch as N. and N. have
consented together in holy
Wedlock, and have witnessed

Then the Minister shall say,

Let us pray.
O Eternal God, Creator and
Preserver of all mankind,
Giver of all spiritual grace,
the Author of everlasting
life; Send thy blessing upon
these thy servants, this Man
and this Woman, whom we bless
in thy Name; that as Isaac
and Rebecca lived faithfully
together, so these persons
may surely perform and keep
the vow and covenant betwixt
them made, and may ever
remain in perfect love and
peace together, and live
according to thy laws,
through Jesus Christ our
Lord. *Amen.*

Then shall the Minister join
their Right Hands together,
and say,
Those whom God hath joined
together, let no man put
asunder.
Then shall the Minister speak
unto the People:
Forasmuch as M. and N. have
consented together in holy
wedlock, and have witnessed

the same before God and this company, and thereto have given and pledged their troth either to other, and have declared the same by giving and receiving of a Ring, and by joining of hands: I pronounce that they are Man and Wife together, In the Name of the Father, and of the Son, and of the Holy Ghost. Amen.

And the Minister shall add this blessing:
God the Father, God the Son, God the Holy Ghost, bless, preserve, and keep you; the Lord mercifully with his favour look upon you, and so fill you with all spiritual benediction and grace, that ye may so live together in this life, that in the world to come ye may have life everlasting. *Amen.*

Then the Minister or Clerks going to the Lords Table, shall say or sing this Psalm following:
Beati omnes. Psalm cxxviii.
Blessed are all they that fear the Lord: and walk in his ways.
For thou shalt eat the labour of thine hands: O well is thee, and happy shalt thou be.
Thy wife shall be as the fruitful vine: upon the walls of thy house.
Thy children like the olive-branches: round about thy table.
Lo, thus shall the man be blessed: that feareth the Lord.
The Lord from out of Sion

the same before God and this company, and thereto have pledged their faith either to other, and have declared the same by joining of hands; I pronounce that they are Man and Wife together, In the Name of the Father, and of the Son, and of the Holy Ghost. *Amen.*

And the Minister shall add this blessing:
God the Father, God the Son, God the Holy Ghost, bless, preserve, and keep you; the Lord mercifully with his favour look upon you, and so fill you with all spiritual benediction and grace, that ye may so live together in this life, that in the world to come ye may have life everlasting. *Amen.*

shall so bless thee: that
thou shalt see Jerusalem in
prosperity all thy life long;
Yea, that thou shalt see thy
childrens children: and peace
upon Israel.
Glory be to the Father, &c.
As it was in the, &c.
Or this Psalm.
Deus mifereatur. Psalm lxvii.
God be merciful unto us, and
bless us: and shew us the
light of his countenance,
and be merciful unto us.
That thy ways may be known
upon earth: thy saving health
among all nations.
Let the people praise thee,
O God: yea, let all the people
praise thee.
O let the nations rejoice
and be glad: for thou shalt
judge the folk righteously,
and govern the nations upon
earth.
Let the people praise thee,
O God: let all the people
praise thee.
Then shall the earth bring
forth her increase: and God,
even our own God, shall give
us his blessing.
God shall bless us; and all
the ends of the world shall
fear him.
Glory be to the Father, &c.
As it was in the, &c.

The Psalm ended, and the Man and the Woman kneeling before the Lords Table, the Priest standing at the Table, and turning towards them, shall say,	*Then the Minister shall say,*
Lord, have mercy upon us. *Answer.* Christ, have mercy upon us. *Minister.* Lord, have mercy	Lord, have mercy upon us. *Answ.* Christ, have mercy upon us. *Minister.* Lord, have mercy

upon us.
Our Father, which art in
heaven; Hallowed be thy Name.
Thy kingdom come. Thy will
be done in earth, as it is in
heaven. Give us this day our
daily bread. And forgive us
our trespasses, as we forgive
them that trespass against
us. And lead us not into
temptation; but deliver us
from evil. Amen.
Minister. O Lord, save thy
servant, and thy handmaid;
Answer. Who put their trust
in thee.
Minister. O Lord, send them help
from thy holy place.
Answer. And evermore defend
them.
Minister. Be unto them a
tower of strength,
Answer. From the face of
their enemy.
Minister. O Lord, hear our
prayer.
Answer. And let our cry come
unto thee.
Minister.
O God of Abraham, God of
Isaac, God of Jacob, bless
these thy servants, and sow
the seed of eternal life in
their hearts; that whatsoever
in thy holy Word they shall
profitably learn, they may
indeed fulfill the same.
Look, O Lord, mercifully upon
them from heaven, and bless
them. And as thou didst send
thy blessing upon Abraham and
Sarah, to their great
comfort; so vouchsafe to send
thy blessing upon these thy
servants, that they obeying
thy will, and alway being in

upon us.
Our Father, who art in
heaven; Hallowed be thy Name;
thy kingdom come; Thy will be
done on earth, as it is in
heaven: Give us this day our
daily bread; And forgive us
our trespasses, as we forgive
them that trespass against
us: And lead us not into
temptation; but deliver us
from evil. *Amen.*
Minister. O Lord, save thy
servant and thy handmaid.
Answer. And let them put
their trust in thee.
Minister. O Lord, send
them help from thy holy place;
Answer. And evermore defend
them.
Minister. Be unto them a
tower of strength,
Answer. From the face of
their enemy.
Minister. O Lord, hear our
prayer;
Answer. And let our cry come
unto thee.
Minister.
O God of Abraham, God of
Isaac, God of Jacob, bless
these thy servants, and sow
the seed of eternal life in
their hearts, that whatsoever
in thy holy Word they shall
profitably learn, they may indeed fulfill the same. Look,
O Lord, mercifully upon them
from heaven, and bless them.
And as thou didst send thy
blessing upon Abraham and
Sarah, to their great
comfort; so vouchsafe to send
thy blessing upon these thy
servants; that they obeying
thy will, and always being in

safety under thy protection,
may abide in thy love unto
their lives end, through
Jesus Christ our Lord. *Amen.*
This Prayer next following
shall be omitted, where the
Woman is past Child-bearing.
O Merciful Lord and heavenly
Father, by whose gracious
gift mankind is increased; We
beseech thee assist with thy
blessing these two persons,
that they may both be
fruitful in procreation of
children, and also live
together so long in godly
love and honesty, that they
may see their children
christianly and virtuously
brought up, to thy praise and
honour, through Jesus Christ
our Lord. *Amen.*
O God, who by thy mighty
power hath made all things of
nothing, who also (after
other things set in order)
didst appoint that out of man
(created after thine own
image and similtude) woman
should take her beginning;
and knitting them together,
didst teach that it should
never be lawful to put
asunder those whom thou by
Matrimony hath made one: O
God, who hast consecrated the
state of Matrimony to such an
excellent mystery, that in it
is signified and represented
the spiritual marriage and
unity betwixt Christ and his
Church; Look mercifully upon
these thy servants, that both
this Man may love his Wife
according to thy Word, (as
Christ did love his Spouse
the Church, who gave himself

safety under thy protection,
may abide in thy love unto
their lives end, through
Jesus Christ our Lord. *Amen.*
This Prayer next following
shall be omitted, where the
Woman is past Child-bearing.
O Merciful Lord and heavenly
Father, by whose gracious
gift mankind is increased; We
beseech thee, assist with thy
blessing these two persons,
that they may both be
fruitful in the procreation
of children, and also live
together so long in godly
love and honesty, that they
may see their children
christianly and virtuously
brought up, to thy praise and
honour, through Jesus Christ
our Lord. *Amen.*
O God, who by thy mighty
power hath made all things of
nothing, who also (after
other things set in order)
didst appoint that out of man
(created after thine own
image and similtude) woman
should take her beginning:
and knitting them together,
didst teach that it should
never be lawful to put
asunder those who thou by
Matrimony hadst made one: O
God, who hast consecrated the
state of Matrimony to such an
excellent mystery, that in it
is signified and represented
the spiritual marriage and
unity betwixt Christ and his
Church; Look mercifully upon
these thy servants, that both
this man may love his wife,
according to thy Word (as
Christ did love his spouse
the Church, who gave himself

for it, loving and cherishing it, even as his own flesh) and also that this Woman may be loving and amiable, faithful and obedient to her Husband, and in all quietness, sobriety, and peace, be a follower of holy and godly matrons. O Lord, bless them both, and grant them to inherit thy everlasting kingdom, through Jesus Christ our Lord. *Amen.*

Then shall the Priest say,

Almighty God, who at the beginning did create our first parents, Adam and Eve, and did sanctify and join them together in marriage; Pour upon you the riches of his grace, sanctify and bless you, that ye may please him both in body and soul, and live together in holy love unto your lives end. *Amen.*

After which, if there be no Sermon declaring the duties of Man and Wife, the Minister shall read as followeth:

All ye that are married, or that intend to take the holy estate of Matrimony upon you, hear what the holy Scripture doth say as touching the duty of Husbands towards their Wives, and Wives towards their Husbands.

Saint Paul in his Epistle to the Ephesians, the fifth Chapter, doth give this commandment to all married men; Husbands, love your Wives, even as Christ also loved the Church, and gave himself for it, that he might sanctify and cleanse it with the washing of water by the Word; that

for it, loving and cherishing it, even as his own flesh), and also that this woman may be loving and amiable, faithful and obedient to her husband: and in all quietness, sobriety, and peace, be a follower of holy and godly matrons. O Lord, bless them both, and grant them to inherit thy everlasting kingdom, through Jesus Christ our Lord. *Amen.*

Then shall the Minister say,

Almighty God, who at the beginning did create our first parents, Adam and Eve, and did sanctify and join them together in marriage; Pour upon you the riches of his grace, sanctify and bless you, that ye may please him both in body and soul, and live together in holy love unto your lives end. *Amen.*[1]

he might present it to himself
a glorious Church, not having
spot or wrinkle, or any such
thing; but that it should
be holy and without blemish.
So ought men to love their
wives as their own bodies:
He that loveth his wife, loveth
himself. For no man ever
yet hateth his own flesh,
but nourisheth and cherisheth
it, even as the Lord the Church:
For we are members of his
body, of his flesh, and of
his bones. For this cause
shall a man leave his father
and mother, and shall be joined
unto his wife, and they two
shall be one flesh. This
is a great mystery; but I
speak concerning Christ and
the Church. Nevertheless,
let every one of you in
particular so love his wife,
even as himself. *Ephes. v.*
25.

Likewise the same Saint
Paul, writing to the Colossians,
speaketh thus to all men that
are married, Husbands, love
your wives, and be not bitter
against them. *Col. iii. 19.*

Hear also what Saint Peter
the Apostle of Christ, who
was himself a married man,
saith unto them that are married,
Ye husbands,
dwell with your wives according
to knowledge, giving honour
unto the wife, as unto the
weaker vessel, and as being
heirs together of the grace
of life, that your prayers
be not hindered. *I.S. Pet.*
iii. 7.

Hitherto ye have heard the
duty of the husband toward
the wife. Now likewise, ye

wives, hear and learn your
duties toward your husbands,
even as it is plainly set
forth in holy Scripture.

Saint Paul, in the aforenamed
Epistle to the Ephesians,
teacheth you thus; Wives,
submit yourselves unto your
own husbands, as unto the
Lord. For the husband is
the head of the wife, even
as Christ is the head of the
Church: and he is the Saviour
of the body. Therefore as
the Church is subject unto
Christ, so let the wives be
to their own husbands in every
thing. And again he saith,
Let the wife see that she
reverence her husband. *Ephes.
v. 22.*

And in his Epistle to the
Colossians Saint Paul giveth
you this short Lesson; Wives
submit yourselves unto your
own husbands, as it is fit
in the Lord. *Col. iii. 18.*

Saint Peter also doth instruct
you very well, thus saying,
Ye wives be in subjection
to your own husbands; that
if any obey not the Word,
they also may without the
Word be won by the conversation
of the wives; while they behold
your chaste conversation coupled
with fear. Whose adorning
let it not be that outward
adorning of plaiting the hair,
and of wearing of gold, or
of putting on of apparel;
but let it be the hidden man
of the heart, in that which
is not corruptible, even the
ornament of a meek and quiet
spirit, which is in the sight
of God of great price. For

after this manner in the old
time the holy women also,
who trusted in God, adorned
themselves, being in subjection
unto their own husbands; even
as Sara obeyed Abraham, calling
him Lord; whose daughters
ye are as long as ye do well,
and are not afraid with any
amazement. *I. S Pet. iii.*
1.
It is convenient that the
new married Persons should
receive the holy Communion
at the time of their Marriage,
or at the first opportunity
after their Marriage.[2]

Appendix B:
Matthew Parker's Table

A TABLE of Kindred *and* Affinity,
wherein whosoever are related, are forbidden
in Scripture, and our Laws, to marry together.

A man may not marry his
1 Grandmother.
2 Grandfathers Wife.
3 Wifes Grandmother.
4 Fathers Sister.
5 Mothers Sister.
6 Fathers Brothers Wife.
7 Mothers Brothers Wife.
8 Wifes Fathers Sister.
9 Wifes Mothers Sister.
10 Mother.
11 Step-Mother.
12 Wifes Mother.
13 Daughter.
14 Wifes Daughter.
15 Sons Wife.
16 Sister.
17 Wifes Sister.
18 Brothers Wife.
19 Sons Daughter.
20 Daughters Daughter.
21 Sons Sons Wife.
22 Daughters Sons Wife.
23 Wifes Sons Daughter.
24 Wifes Daughters Daughter.
25 Brothers Daughter.
26 Sisters Daughter.
27 Brothers Sons Wife.
28 Sisters Sons Wife.
29 Wifes Brothers Daughter.
30 Wifes Sisters Daughter.

A Woman may not marry her
1 Grandfather.
2 Grandmothers Husband.
3 Husbands Grandfather.
4 Fathers Brother.
5 Mothers Brother.
6 Fathers Sisters Husband.
7 Mothers Sisters Husband.
8 Husbands Fathers Brother.
9 Husbands Mothers Brother.
10 Father.
11 Step-Father.
12 Husbands Father.
13 Son.
14 Husbands Son.
15 Daughters Husband.
16 Brother.
17 Husbands Brother.
18 Sisters Husband.
19 Sons Son.
20 Daughters Son.
21 Sons Daughters Husband.
22 Daughters Daughters Husband.
23 Husbands Sons Son.
24 Husbands Daughters Son.
25 Brothers Son.
26 Sisters Son.
27 Brothers Daughters Husband.
28 Sisters Daughters Husband.
29 Husbands Brothers Son.
30 Husbands Sisters Son.[1]

Notes

Introduction

1. Wesley F. Swift, "Methodism and The Book of Common Prayer," *Proceedings of The Wesley Historical Society* 27 (1949–50): 34.

2. Frank Baker, *John Wesley and the Church of England* (Nashville, Tenn.: Abingdon Press, 1970), 244.

3. *The Works of John Wesley*, 3d ed., 14 vols., ed. Thomas Jackson (London: Wesleyan Methodist Book Room, 1872; reprint, Grand Rapids, Mich.: Baker Book House, 1984), 12:438.

4. Nolan B. Harmon, Jr., "John Wesley's 'Sunday Service' and Its American Revisions," *Proceedings of The Wesley Historical Society* 39 (June 1974): 137.

Chapter 1. "I Publish the Banns of Marriage"

1. Frank Baker, "John Wesley's First Marriage," *The Duke Divinity School Review* 31 (autumn 1966): 176.

2. Evan Daniel, *The Prayer-Book: Its History, Language, and Contents*, 22nd ed. (London: Wells Gardner, Darton & Co., 1909), 493.

3. John R. Gillis, *For Better, For Worse: British Marriages, 1600 to the Present* (New York: Oxford University Press, 1985), 17.

4. Michel Despland, "Norms and Models in Early Modern France and England: A Study in Comparative Ethics," *The Journal of Religious Ethics* 10 (spring 1982): 81.

5. Gillis, *For Better, For Worse*, 136.

6. Despland, "Norms and Models," 81.

7. J. G. Davies, ed., *The New Westminster Dictionary of Liturgy and Worship* (Philadelphia: Westminster Press, 1986) s.v. "Marriage: Medieval and Roman Catholic," by J. D. Crichton.

8. Robert Gregorio, "A History of Christian Marriage," *Liturgy* 4, no. 2 (spring 1984): 40.

9. Ibid., 43.

10. Richard Burn, *Ecclesiastical Law* (London, 1763), 2:16–19, quoted in Baker, "John Wesley's First Marriage," 176.

11. Lawrence Stone, *The Family, Sex and Marriage in England 1500–1800* (New York: Harper & Row, 1977), 32.

12. Henry Swinburne, *A Treatise of Spousals or Matrimonial Contracts: Wherein All the Questions relating to the Subject are ingeniously Debated and Resolved* (London: S. Roycroft for Robert Clavell, 1686), iv–v, 13.

13. John Goole, *The Contract Violated* (London, 1734), App. 2–4, quoted in Baker, "John Wesley's First Marriage," 182.

14. Swinburne, *A Treatise of Spousals*, 114.

15. *A Treatise of Femme Coverts: or, the Lady's Law Containing All the Laws and*

Statutes relating to Women (London: E. & R. Nutt & R. Gosling, for B. Lintot, 1732), 29, 31.

16. F. E. Brightman, *The English Rite: Being a Synopsis of the Sources and Revisions of The Book of Common Prayer with an Introduction and an Appendix*, 2 vols. (London: Rivingtons, 1915), 2:802.

17. Kenneth Stevenson, *Nuptial Blessing: A Study of Christian Marriage Rites* (New York: Oxford University Press, 1983), 135.

18. Brightman, *English Rite*, 2:802.

19. Nolan B. Harmon, Jr., *The Rites and Ritual of Episcopal Methodism: With Particular Reference to the Rituals of the Methodist Episcopal Church and the Methodist Episcopal Church, South, Respectively* (Nashville, Tenn.: Publishing House of the M. E. Church, South, 1926), 250. See appendix A for a comparison of Wesley's service and the 1662 *Book of Common Prayer*.

20. Daniel, *Prayer Book*, 491.

21. Harmon, Jr., *Rites and Ritual*, 263.

22. W. K. Lowther Clarke and Charles Harris, ed., *Liturgy and Worship: A Companion to the Prayer Books of the Anglican Communion* (New York: Macmillan Co., 1932), 463.

23. Brightman, *English Rite*, 2:800.

24. Ibid., 2:801.

25. Clarke and Harris, *Liturgy and Worship*, 464.

26. Henri Misson, *Memoirs and Observations in His Travels over England (1697)* (London, 1719), 183, quoted in Gillis, *For Better, For Worse*, 137.

27. Stone, *Family, Sex and Marriage*, 33.

28. Willystine Goodsell, *A History of Marriage and the Family*, rev. ed. (New York: Macmillan Co., 1934), 335.

29. Stone, *Family, Sex and Marriage*, 33.

30. John H. Overton and Frederic Relton, *The English Church: From the Accession of George I. to the End of the Eighteenth Century (1714–1800)* (London: Macmillan & Co., 1906), 297.

31. Bernard I. Murstein, *Love, Sex, and Marriage Through the Ages*, with a foreword by William M. Kephart (New York: Spring Publishing Co., 1974), 225.

32. Stone, *Family, Sex and Marriage*, 33.

33. T. A. Lacey, *Marriage in Church and State*, fully revised and supplemented by R. C. Mortimer (London: S.P.C.K., 1959), 165.

34. Goodsell, *Marriage and Family*, 333.

35. Ibid., 382–84.

36. *Journals and Diaries I (1735–38)*, vol. 18 of *The Works of John Wesley* ed. by W. Reginald Ward and Richard P. Heitzenrater (Nashville: Abingdon Press, 1988), 419.

37. Ibid., 498.

38. Ibid., 501.

39. Charles Wesley, *The Journal of the Rev. Charles Wesley, M.A.: Sometimes Student of Christ Church, Oxford, to Which Are Appended Selections from His Correspondence and Poetry*, with an introduction and occasional Notes by Thomas Jackson, 2 vols. (London: John Mason, 1849), 2:54.

40. *The Journal of the Rev. John Wesley, A.M.: Enlarged from Original Mss. with Notes from Unpublished Diaries, Annotations, Maps, and Illustrations*, ed. Nehemiah Curnock (London: Epworth Press, 1938), 3:512–13.

41. James F. White, introduction to *John Wesley's Prayer Book: The Sunday*

Service of the Methodists in North America, by John Wesley (Cleveland: OSL Publications, 1991), 1.

42. Wesley, *Sunday Service,* 2. This and future reference to the *Sunday Service* are to the 1784 edition reprinted by The United Methodist Publishing House in 1992.

43. Bard Thompson, *Liturgies of the Western Church* (Philadelphia: Fortress Press, 1961), 411.

44. Harmon, *Rites and Ritual,* 250.

45. Clarke and Harris, *Liturgy and Worship,* 465.

46. Stanley Ayling, *John Wesley* (Nashville, Tenn.: Abingdon Press, 1979), 222–23.

47. Ibid., 223–24.

48. John Wesley, *Explanatory Notes upon the Old Testament* (Bristol: William Pine, 1765; reprint, Salem, Ohio: Schmul Publishers, 1975), 1:116.

49. Ibid., 2:879.

50. John Wesley, *Explanatory Notes upon the New Testament* (London: The Wesleyan-Methodist Book-Room, n.d.; reprint, Grand Rapids: Baker Book House, 1986), Mark 10:11–12. These *Notes* have no page numbers but are arranged under the biblical citation.

51. Ibid., 1 Cor. 7:2. Unless otherwise indicated, biblical quotations are from the King James Version.

52. *The Letters of the Rev. John Wesley, A.M.,* ed. John Telford, 8 vols. (London: Epworth Press, 1931), 7:106.

53. Lacey, *Church and State,* 159.

54. Francis Procter, *A New History of "The Book of Common Prayer,"* revised and rewritten by Walter Howard Frere (London: Macmillan & Co., 1955), 621.

55. Clarke and Harris, *Liturgy and Worship,* 470.

56. "Constitutions and Canons Ecclesiastical," in *Certain Sermons: Appointed by the Queen's Majesty to Be Declared and Read by All Parsons, Vicars, and Curates, Every Sunday and Holiday in Their Churches; and by Her Grace's Advice Perused and Overseen for the Better Understanding of the Simple People* (Cambridge: John W. Parker, 1850), 667. For Parker's table, see appendix B.

57. Wesley, *Journal,* 4:187.

58. Ibid., 7:125–26.

59. White, introduction to *Wesley's Prayer Book,* 31.

60. Clarke and Harris, *Liturgy and Worship,* 465.

61. Lacey, *Church and State,* 166–67.

62. Stone, *Family, Sex and Marriage,* 35.

63. Daniel, *Prayer Book* 492.

64. Lacey, *Church and State,* 167.

65. Clarke and Harris, 463.

66. Stone, *Family, Sex, and Marriage,* 36.

67. Lacey, *Church and State,* 167.

68. George Hayward Joyce, *Christian Marriage: An Historical and Doctrinal Study,* 2d ed. rev. and enl. (London: Sheed & Ward, 1948), 143.

69. Overton and Relton, *The English Church,* 297.

70. Samuel Pyeatt Menefee, *Wives for Sale: An Ethnographic Study of British Popular Divorce* (New York: St. Martin's Press, 1981), 11.

71. Dafydd Ifans, "Lewis Morris ac Afrerion Piodi yng Ngherdigion," *Ceredigion* 8, no. 2 (1972): 251, quoted in John R. Gillis, "Married But Not Churched:

Plebian Sexual Relations and Marital Nonconformity in Eighteenth-Century Britain," *Eighteenth Century Life*, n.s., 9, no. 3 (May 1985): 35.

72. Goodsell, *Marriage and Family*, 384–89.

73. Frederick A. Norwood, ed., *The Methodist Discipline of 1798: Including the Annotations of Thomas Coke and Francis Asbury*, (Rutland, Vt.: Academy Books, 1979), 54–55, 58–68, 115–17.

74. On the whole story of John Goole and Margaret Hudson, see Baker, "John Wesley's First Marriage," 179–83.

75. For Wesley's own account of his relationship with Grace Murray, see his diary in J. A. Leger, *John Wesley's Last Love* (London: J. M. Dent & Sons, 1910), 1–105.

76. Baker, "John Wesley's First Marriage," 187–88.

77. Frederick E. Maser, "John Wesley's Only Marriage: An Examination of Dr. Frank Baker's Article 'John Wesley's First Marriage,'" *Methodist History* 16 (October 1977): 33–41.

78. Wesley, *Old Testament*, 2:1002.

79. William Henry Meredith, *The Real John Wesley* (Cincinnati, Ohio: Jennings & Pye, 1903), 325.

80. Henry Moore, *Life of John Wesley*, First English edition, 2:171, quoted in Meredith, *The Real John Wesley*, 326–27.

81. Leger, *Wesley's Last Love*, 98–105.

Chapter 2. "At the Day and Time Appointed"

1. Wesley, *Sunday Service*, 149.

2. Brightman, *English Rite*, 2:800–801, emphasis added.

3. Gillis, *For Better, For Worse*, 86.

4. Kenneth Stevenson, "Marriage Liturgy: Lessons from History," *Anglican Theological Review* 68 (July 1986): 235.

5. Clarke and Harris, *Liturgy and Worship*, 465.

6. Stone, *Family, Sex, and Marriage*, 35.

7. Wesley, *Journal*, 1:60, 247, 287, 307, 311, 343, 357.

8. Clarke and Harris, *Liturgy and Worship*, 464.

9. Richard Hooker, *Of the Laws of Ecclesiastical Polity* (London: J. M. Dent & Sons, 1922), 392–93.

10. Procter, *New History* 620. Convocation is "an assembly of the clergy of the Church of England . . . called together to consult on ecclesiastical affairs." See Jerald C. Brauer, *The Westminster Dictionary of Church History* (Philadelphia Westminster Press, 1971), s. v. "Convocation."

11. Wesley, *Journals and Diaries I*, 458, 493, 510. Wesley notes in his diary that Easter was 10 April that year (1737).

12. Wesley, *Sunday Service*, 2–3.

13. Charles Wesley, *Journal*, 2:55.

14. Wesley, *Journal*, 3:513.

15. Wesley, *Sunday Service*, 149.

16. Brightman, *English Rite*, 2:816–17, emphasis added.

17. Harmon, *Rites and Ritual*, 260.

18. Kenneth Stevenson, *Nuptial Blessing*, 139.

19. E. C. Whitaker, *Martin Bucer and The Book of Common Prayer* (Great Wakering, England: Mayhew-McCrimmon, 1974), 124.

20. Hooker, *Ecclesiastical Polity*, 396–97.

21. Ibid., 396.

22. Ibid., 397.

23. Procter, *New History*, 619.

24. Ibid.

25. Ibid.

26. Kenneth Stevenson, *Nuptial Blessing*, 145.

27. John C. Bowmer, *The Sacrament of the Lord's Supper in Early Methodism* (Westminster, England: Dacre Press, 1951), 7.

28. Wesley, *Journals and Diaries I*, 403, 458, 493. In contrast to the prevailing Anglican custom, John Wesley strongly believed in a weekly celebration of the Lord's Supper. See page 43.

29. Charles Wesley, *Journal*, 2:55.

30. Ayling, *John Wesley*, 232.

31. Charles Wesley, *Journal*, 2:56. It is not assuming too much to see allusions to the Eucharist in these eschatological references to Christ as "our Bridegroom" and to the heavenly marriage feast. In fact, this was a common theme in the eucharistic hymns of the Wesley brothers. See Ole E. Borgen, *John Wesley on the Sacraments* (Grand Rapids, Mich.: Francis Asbury Press, 1972), 217–34, and J. Ernest Rattenbury, *The Eucharistic Hymns of John and Charles Wesley* (London: Epworth Press, 1948), 61–78.

32. White, introduction to *Wesley's Prayer Book*, 25.

33. Kenneth Stevenson, *Nuptial Blessing*, 158.

34. Wesley, *Works*, 7:148.

35. Wesley, *Sunday Service*, ii.

36. Ibid.

37. Baker, *Church of England*, 332–33.

38. See page 27 for a discussion of who was permitted to preside at marriage services in the early years of American independence.

39. Leighton Pullan, *The History of "The Book of Common Prayer"* (London: Longmans, Green, & Co., 1914), 219.

40. Brightman, *English Rite*, 2:800–801.

41. James F. White, introduction to *John Wesley's Sunday Service of the Methodists of North America* (Nashville: United Methodist Publishing House, 1984), 24.

42. Paul Neff Garber, *The Methodist Meeting House* (New York: Board of Missions and Church Extension, The Methodist Church, 1941), 17–21.

43. Ibid., 16, 27. For a more detailed discussion of early Methodist church architecture in the United States, see Garber passim; James F. White, *Protestant Worship and Church Architecture: Theological and Historical Considerations* (New York: Oxford University Press, 1964), 112–16; James F. White, "Early Methodist Liturgical Architecture," *Motive* 18 (March 1958): 12–13, 19–20.

44. White, introduction to *Wesley's Prayer Book*, 2.

45. Brightman, *English Rite*, 2:800–801, emphasis added.

46. Charles Wesley, *Journal*, 2:55.

47. Wesley, *Journal*, 4:361.

48. Daniel, *Prayer Book*, 492.

49. Stevenson, "Marriage Liturgy," 228.

50. Donald M. Scott and Bernard Wishy, eds., *America's Families: A Documentary History* (New York: Harper & Row, 1982), 76, emphasis added.

51. Wesley, *Works*, 3:251.

52. William Nash Wade, "A History of Public Worship in the Methodist

Episcopal Church and Methodist Episcopal Church, South, from 1784 to 1905"
(Ph.D. dis., University of Notre Dame, 1981), 249–52.

53. Brightman, *English Rite*, 2:815.

54. White, introduction to *Wesley's Prayer Book*, 25.

55. Stevenson, "Marriage Liturgy," 235.

56. Wesley, *Works*, 8:317. The Large Minutes, a compilation of the decisions of the Methodist conferences between 1744 and 1789, formed the plan of discipline for the Methodists during Wesley's lifetime.

57. Norwood, *Discipline*, 84–85. Wesley himself, of course, wrote many original sermons which became models for other Methodist preachers. See *Wesley's Standard Sermons*, ed. Edward H. Sugden, 3d ed. Annotated, 2 vols. (London: Epworth Press, 1951).

58. White, introduction to *Wesley's Prayer Book*, 12.

59. Baker, *Church of England*, 328.

60. White, introduction to *Wesley's Prayer Book*, 24.

61. Charles J. Abbey and John H. Overton, *The English Church in the Eighteenth Century* (London: Longmans, Green, & Co., 1896), 458.

62. Russel N. Squire, *Church Music: Musical and Hymnological Developments in Western Christianity* (St. Louis, Mo: Bethany Press, 1962), 197–98.

63. John Wesley, "An Unpublished Wesley Letter," *Proceedings of The Wesley Historical Society* 39 (June 1974): 144.

64. Wesley, *Works*, 8:319.

65. Wade, "History of Public Worship," 67–68, 76.

66. Wesley, *Works*, 2:226.

67. Ibid., 3:111.

68. Ibid., 4:223.

69. Ibid.

70. Ibid., 13:470–73.

71. Ibid., 8:318.

72. Norwood, *Discipline*, 123–34.

73. White, introduction to *Wesley's Prayer Book*, 1–2.

74. Wesley, *Works*, 3:160–61.

75. Ibid., 3:339.

76. Ibid.

77. Ibid., 4:200.

78. Abbey and Overton, *The English Church*, 456–58.

79. Wesley, *Works*, 10:445.

80. Ibid, 13:217.

81. Baker, *Church of England*, 339.

82. Meredith, *The Real John Wesley*, 323.

Chapter 3. "The Causes for Matrimony"

1. White, introduction to *Wesley's Prayer Book*, 24.

2. Kenneth Stevenson, *Nuptial Blessing*, 135.

3. James Turner Johnson, *A Society Ordained by God: English Puritan Marriage Doctrine in the First Half of the Seventeenth Century*, Studies in Christian Ethics Series (Nashville, Tenn.: Abingdon Press, 1970), 22.

4. Hooker, *Ecclesiastical Polity*, 391.

5. Ibid.

6. Johnson, *Society Ordained by God*, 45.

7. Wesley, *Works*, 10:154. See also 10:127.

8. Wesley, *Old Testament*, 1:13.

9. Johnson, *Society Ordained by God*, 21.

10. Ibid., 117.

11. Whitaker, *Martin Bucer*, 120–22.

12. Despland, "Norms and Models," 82–84. It is ironic that today, people who regard sex primarily as a means of reproduction and minimize its value as a source of enjoyment for the partners are popularly labeled "Puritanical." For, as the preceding statements show, historically speaking, such an attitude is not Puritanical at all, but Episcopalian!

13. Johnson, *Society Ordained by God*, 47.

14. Bertha Katschke-Jennings, "Some Church Historical Perspectives on Divorce and Remarriage," *American Baptist Quarterly* 3 (March 1984): 49.

15. Menefee, *Wives for Sale*, 23. It may surprise some readers that the Anglican Church retained the Roman Catholic teaching about divorce, since it was the desire of Henry VIII to be free of a wife that occasioned the split between Canterbury and Rome in the first place! But strictly speaking, what Henry sought was not a divorce, but an annulment on the grounds that it had been unlawful for him to marry his brother's widow. (Several decades later, Matthew Parker's table would support Henry's position. See pages 24–25 and appendix B.) Parliament had to pass a series of laws over the following years to accommodate the king's wishes regarding his successive wives. See Lacey, *Church and State*, 157–59.

16. Robert C. Monk, *John Wesley: His Puritan Heritage* (Nashville, Tenn.: Abingdon Press, 1966), 186.

17. Stone, *Family, Sex, and Marriage*, 37.

18. Ibid., 38.

19. Ibid., 40. The courts made "intermittent and half-hearted attempts" to stop this practice, but it did not disappear completely until 1887!

20. Katschke-Jennings, "Historical Perspectives," 47–48.

21. Charmarie Jenkins Blaisdell, "The Matrix of Reform: Women in Lutheran and Calvinist Movements," in *Triumph Over Silence: Women in Protestant History*, ed. Richard L. Greaves (Westport, Conn.: Greenwood Press, 1985), 41–42.

22. Katschke-Jennings, "Historical Perspectives," 48.

23. *The Works of John Milton* (New York: Columbia University Press, 1931), 4:97.

24. Ibid., 15:171.

25. Wesley, *Works*, 5:280.

26. Wesley, *Old Testament*, 1:655–56.

27. Wesley, *New Testament*, Matthew 19:7, 9. The excerpts from Wesley's writings quoted here were selected because they present a clear, concise statement of Wesley's teaching on divorce. Wesley also comments on divorce in *Thoughts on Marriage and a Single Life*, (Bristol: Felix Farley, 1743) 5–6; *Old Testament*, 1:406, 3:2609; and *New Testament*, Matt. 5:31–32, 19:4, and 1 Cor. 7:11, 12, 15.

28. Brightman, *English Rite*, 2:806; Thompson, *Liturgies*, 230. Hermann's original text for the proclamation of marriage read as follows: "Weil dan Hans N. vnd Anna N. einander zur Ehe begeren, auch die Ehe einander versprochen, vnd solche hie offentlich fur Gott vn seiner Genein bekennet, daran H die hende vnd Trew Ring ein ander gegeben haben. So spreche ich sie Ehelich zusamen, vnd bestatige ire Ehe im namen des Vatters, vnd des Sons, vn des H. Geiste, Amen." Forasmuch as Hans N. and Anna N. desire one another in marriage,

have also promised marriage to one another, and confess the same here publicly before God and his community, therefore they have given hands and a wedding ring to one another. Thus I pronounce them joined in marriage, and I confirm their marriage in the name of the Father, and of the Son, and of the Holy Spirit, Amen.

29. Brightman, *English Rite*, 2:801.
30. Kenneth Stevenson, *Nuptial Blessing*, 141.
31. Leger, *Wesley's Last Love*, 66–68.
32. Wesley, *Thoughts on Marriage*, 8–9.
33. Ibid., 6–7.
34. Leger, *Wesley's Last Love*, 1. It was only two months after this conference that Wesley first spoke to Grace Murray of his interest in marrying her!
35. Wesley, *Works*, 11:457.
36. Ibid., 11:458.
37. Ibid., 11:462.
38. Wesley, *New Testament*, Matt. 19:12.
39. Wesley, *New Testament*, 1 Cor. 7:7.
40. Wesley, *Journal*, 3:512.
41. Wesley, *Letters*, 7:65.
42. Ayling, *John Wesley*, 30.
43. Included by John Wesley, in *A Christian Library: Consisting of Extracts from and Abridgements of the Choicest Pieces of Practical Divinity Which Have Been Published in the English Tongue*, 30 vols., (London: T. Cordeux, 1821), 9:157.
44. Wesley, *Works*, 11:458–60.
45. Ibid., 11:459.
46. Wesley, *Works*, 11:464–65. Wesley also speaks of the benefits of the single life in his *New Testament* commentary, Matt. 11:37; 22:30, Luke 14:26, and 1 Cor. 7:26–34.
47. Leger, *Wesley's Last Love*, 83.
48. Wesley, *Letters*, 6:270–71.
49. Ibid., 6:70.
50. Charles Wesley Flint, *Charles Wesley and His Colleagues*, with introductory notes by Gerald Kennedy, G. Bromley Oxnam, and Norman Vincent Peale (Washington, D.C.: Public Affairs Press, 1957), 70.
51. Wesley, *Works*, 11:460.
52. Ibid. Jeremy Taylor had also recommended prayer as an important part of resisting sexual temptation. See Wesley, *Christian Library*, 9:163.
53. Wesley, *Works*, 11:460. See Jeremy Taylor's comments in Wesley, *Christian Library*, 9:163.
54. Wesley, *Works*, 11:461. For Jeremy Taylor's thoughts, see Wesley, *Christian Library*, 9:162–63.
55. Wesley, *Old Testament*, 2:878.
56. John Wesley, *Thoughts on the Sin of Onan* (London, 1767), 3–20. Wesley regarded himself as something of an amateur physician and published a widely read book of home remedies called *Primitive Physick*. See Ayling, *John Wesley*, 167–69.
57. Wesley, *Works*, 11:461–62.
58. Wesley, *Old Testament*, 2:1023. See Jeremy Taylor's comments in Wesley, *Christian Library*, 9:162.
59. Wesley, *Christian Library*, 9:157.
60. Ibid., 29:122.

61. Wesley, *Thoughts on Marriage*, 3.
62. Wesley, *Works*, 8:341.
63. Leger, *John Wesley*, 68–70.
64. Ibid., 74. The word "intercourse," in this context, means, of course, "interaction."
65. Wesley, *Journal*, 3:512.
66. Wesley, *Works*, 12:207.
67. Wesley, *Letters*, 7:175–76.
68. Wesley, *Works*, 13:109–110.
69. Ibid., 11:456–57.
70. Wesley, *New Testament*, 1 Cor. 7:3–4.
71. Wesley, *Old Testament*, 1:383.
72. Wesley, *New Testament*, 1 Cor. 7:5. Jeremy Taylor and William Whateley had also taught that the "due and lawful enjoyment of marriage" was of great help in avoiding forbidden sexual activities. See Wesley, *Christian Library*, 9:163, 12:261.
73: Wesley, *Old Testament*, 3:1839. Wesley does not explain what he means by "excess in the marriage bed," but other writers are more explicit. See Wesley, *Christian Library*, 4:383–84, 8:82, 9:160–61, 12:264–65.
74. Lacey, *Church and State*, 161.
75. Steven Ozment, *The Age of Reform 1250–1550: An Intellectual and Religious History of Late Medieval and Reformation Europe* (New Haven: Yale University Press, 1980), 395.
76. Anne Llewellyn Barstow, "An Ambiguous Legacy: Anglian Clergy Wives after the Reformation," in *Women in New Worlds: Historical Perspectives on the Wesleyan Tradition*, ed. Rosemary Skinner Keller, Louise L. Queen, and Hilah F. Thomas, vol. 2 (Nashville: Abingdon, 1982), 99.
77. Wesley, *Works*, 10:154–55. Wesley said substantially the same thing in "A Roman Catechism" and "Thoughts on a Single Life." See Wesley, *Works*, 10:128, 11:456–57.
78. Wesley, *New Testament Notes*, Heb. 13:4.
79. Ibid, Tit. 1:6.
80. Ibid., 1 Tim. 4:3.
81. Wesley, *Old Testament*, 2:1194.
82. Wesley, *Journal*, 8:151–52.
83. Wesley, *Letters*, 5:62–63. The couple in question did, in fact, marry, and lived together happily.
84. Ibid., 7:154.
85. Ibid., 8:116.
86. Wesley, *Works*, 8:309, 325.
87. Ibid., 13:72.
88. John Wesley, "Unpublished Letters of John Wesley," *Methodist History* 1 (October 1962): 37.
89. Leger, *Wesley's Last Love*, 1.
90. John Pawson, "Extracts from Letters of the Revd. John Pawson. 1762–1806," *Proceedings of The Wesley Historical Society* 11 (1918): 51.
91. Meredith, *The Real John Wesley*, 341.
92. Wesley, *Journal*, 3:517.
93. Ayling, *John Wesley*, 230–31.
94. Ibid., 226.

95. Wesley's account of this period of his life (as presented in this section) can be found in his *Journals and Diaries I*, 365–71, 430–42, 461–88.

96. Wesley, *Letters*, 1:199. The fact that Wesley wrote these sentences in Greek rather than English is indicative of the confidential nature of this confession.

97. Alan L. Hayes, "John Wesley and Sophy Hopkey: A Case Study in Wesley's Attitude Toward Woman," in Keller, Queen, and Thomas, *Women in New Worlds*, 42. Obviously, psychological as well as theological considerations were influencing Wesley's behavior in his relationships with women. For a psychological examination of Wesley's ideas and actions, see Robert L. Moore, *John Wesley and Authority: A Psychological Perspective*, American Academy of Religion Dissertation Series, no. 29 (Ann Arbor, Mich.: Edwards Bros., 1979).

98. L. David Miller, *Hymns: The Story of Christian Song* (Philadelphia: Lutheran Church Press, 1969), 95.

99. John L. Nuelsen, *John Wesley and the German Hymn*, trans. Theo Parry, Sydney H. Moore, and Arthur Holbrook (Calverly, England: A. S. Holbrook, 1972), 61–63. Tersteegen's original German text of this stanza reads as follows:

> Ist etwas das ich neben dir
> in aller welt wolt lieben?
> Ach! nimm es hin, bis nichts in mir
> als du seyst uberblieben:
> ich weisz, ich musz von allem losz,
> eh ich in deinem friedens-schnoosz
> kan bleiben ohne wancken.

Chapter 4. "Who Gyves Me This Wyfe?"

1. Hooker, *Ecclesiastical Polity*, 393.

2. Gillis, *For Better, For Worse*, 18.

3. Brightman, *English Rite*, 2:804–5.

4. Wesley, *Old Testament*, 1:13. Wesley makes the same point in his comments on Exod. 22:17, Num. 30:5, and Judg. 14:2.

5. Wesley, *Works*, 12:359.

6. Wesley, *Letters*, 5:109.

7. Ibid., 7:83–84.

8. Ibid., 8:28–29.

9. Ibid., 8:35.

10. Wesley, *Journal*, 8:150.

11. Frank Baker, *Charles Wesley: As Revealed by His Letters* (London: Epworth Press, 1948), 60, 63–66.

12. Wesley, *Works*, 8:308.

13. Norwood, *Discipline*, 157. The word "exception" is changed to "exceptions," making it clear that the circumstances cited are intended as two separate examples and not as one compound situation. Also, the last sentence is changed to read, "Yet even then a Methodist preacher ought not to be married to her." This makes it clear that the rule does not prohibit a Methodist preacher from presiding at such a wedding.

14. Despland, "Norms and Models," 81.

15. Wesley, *Old Testament*, 1:95–96.

16. Wesley, *Old Testament*, 1:90.

17. Wesley, *Works*, 7:85. Wesley was equally adamant about this subject in his sermon "On a Single Eye." See Wesley, *Works*, 7:302–3.

18. Stone, *Family, Sex, and Marriage*, 272, 263.

19. Gillis, "Married But Not Churched," 31.

20. Gillis, *For Better, For Worse*, 60.

21. Wesley, *Journal*, 4:361.

22. Charles Wesley, *Journal*, 2:55.

23. Gillis, *For Better, For Worse*, 150.

24. Stone, *Family, Sex, and Marriage*, 55–56.

25. Gillis, *For Better, For Worse*, 18.

26. Whitaker, 122.

27. Wesley, *Works*, 13:29.

28. Ibid., 11:464.

29. Wesley, *Letters*, 6:309.

30. Wesley, *New Testament*, 1 Cor. 7:20.

31. Wesley, *Old Testament*, 1:93.

32. Ibid., 1:113–14.

33. Ibid., 3:1865.

34. Wesley, *Journals and Diaries I*, 176.

35. Leger, *Wesley's Last Love*, 105.

36. Wesley, *Journal*, 3:515.

37. Wesley, *Works*, 12:486.

38. Ibid., 12:485.

39. Ibid., 6:456–57.

40. Wesley, *Old Testament*, 1:607, 2:880, 1451.

41. Wesley, *New Testament*, 1 Cor. 7:39, 2 Cor. 6:14.

42. Wesley, *Works*, 8:308.

43. Wesley, *New Testament*, 1 Cor. 7:14.

44. Wesley, *Letters*, 5:108.

45. Ibid., 5:254.

46. Ibid., 6:72.

47. Ibid., 279–80.

48. Wesley, *Works*, 13:109.

49. Wesley, *Old Testament*, 3:1889.

50. Ibid., 3:1892.

51. Muirstein, *Love, Sex, and Marriage*, 227.

52. Leger, *Wesley's Last Love*, 76.

53. Ibid., 61–62.

54. Ibid., 62.

55. Baker, *Charles Wesley*, 59.

56. Leger, *Wesley's Last Love*, 66.

57. Ibid., 79.

58. Wesley, *Journal*, 3:512–14.

59. Wesley, *Journals and Diaries I*, 467.

60. Wesley, *Letters*, 7:201.

61. Gillis, *For Better, For Worse*, 17.

62. Daniel, *Prayer Book*, 494.

63. Pullan, "Book of Common Prayer," 222–23.

64. Brightman, *English Rite*, 2:804.

65. Pullan, "Book of Common Prayer," 223.

66. Brightman, *English Rite*, 2:804, 806.

67. Ibid., 2:805, 807.

68. Ibid.

69. Whitaker, *Martin Bucer*, 122, 124.

70. Thompson, *Liturgies* 312.

71. Paul Elmen, "On Worshiping the Bride," *Anglican Theological Review* 68 (July 1986): 242.

72. Hooker, *Ecclesiastical Polity*, 395.

73. Elmen, "Worshiping the Bride," 242.

74. Hooker, *Ecclesiastical Polity*, 395.

75. White, introduction to *Wesley's Prayer Book*, 25.

76. Harmon, *Rites and Ritual*, 268.

77. I. A. Muirhead, "'The Forme of Marriage': 1562 and Today," *Scottish Journal of Theology* 6 (1953): 34; Nolan B. Harmon, Jr., "John Wesley's 'Sunday Service' and Its American Revision," *Proceedings of The Wesley Historical Society* 39, (June 1974): 138. James T. Johnson links the absence of a ring with the Puritan understanding of the nature of marriage when he says that the lack of a ring in Puritan weddings signifies "that husband and wife are true partners in marriage, and the wife is no longer merely the husband's chattel" ("English Puritan Thought on the Ends of Marriage," *Church History* 38 [December 1969]: 435).

78. Frederick Hunter, "Sources of Wesley's Revision of The Prayer Book in 1784-8," in *Proceedings of the Wesley Historical Society* 23 (1941–42): 123–33.

79. Harmon, Jr., *Rites and Ritual*, 268; Frederick Hunter, "Sources of Wesley's Revision of the Prayer Book in 1784–8," *Proceedings of The Wesley Historical Society* 23 (1941–42): 123–33; Paul W. Hoon, "The Order for the Service of Marriage," in *Companion to "The Book of Worship,"* ed. William F. Dunkle, Jr. and Joseph D. Quillian, Jr. (Nashville, Tenn.: Abingdon Press, 1970), 75; J. G. Davies, ed., *The New Westminster Dictionary of Liturgy and Worship* (Philadelphia: Westminster Press, 1986) s.v. "Marriage: Methodist," by James F. White, 360.

80. *A Service of Christian Marriage: With Introduction, Commentary, and Additional Resources* (Nashville, Tenn.: United Methodist Publishing House, 1979), 12; *Companion to "The Book of Services": Introduction, Commentary, and Instruction for Using the New United Methodist Services* (Nashville, Tenn.: Abingdon Press, 1988), 97.

81. Karen Westerfield Tucker, "Liturgical Expressions of Care for the Poor in the Wesleyan Tradition: A Case Study for the Ecumenical Church," *Worship* 69 (1995): 55.

82. Wesley, *Works*, 11:468, 8:270, 274. See also Wesley's sermon "On Dress," *Works*, 7:15–26.

83. Wesley, *Works*, 7:64.

84. Thompson, *Liturgies*, 413; Wade, "History of Public Worship", 85.

85. Norwood, *Discipline*, 119.

86. Baker, *Church of England*, 255.

Chapter 5. "The Holy Estate of Matrimony"

1. William Haller and Malleville Haller, "The Puritan Art of Love," *The Huntington Library Quarterly* 5 (January 1942): 267.

2. Richard Green, *The Works of John and Charles Wesley: A Bibliography*, 2d ed. (London: Methodist Publishing House, 1906), 81–82.

3. John Wesley, *Christian Library*, 12:253.

4. Wesley, *Letters*, 7:166.

5. Green, *Bibliography*, 62, 81.

6. Wesley, *Old Testament*, 1:13.

7. Wesley, *New Testament*, 1 Cor. 11:3.

8. Ibid., Mark 10:6.

9. Ibid., 1 Cor. 11:12.

10. Ibid., 1 Cor. 11:11.

11. Ibid., 1 Pet. 3:7.

12. Alan L. Hayes, "John Wesley and Sophy Hopkey," 38–39. See also Earl Kent Brown, *Women of Mr. Wesley's Methodism*, Studies in Women and Religion, vol. 11 (New York: Edwin Mellen Press, 1983).

13. Wesley, *Old Testament*, 2:1061.

14. Brightman, *English Rite*, 2:804–5.

15. Ibid. "Bonere" means gracious and gentle (as in the related word "debonair"); "buxom" means obedient. See Daniel, *Prayer Book*, 493–94.

16. Ibid., 2:810–13.

17. Wesley, *Old Testament*, 1:18.

18. Wesley, *New Testament*, Eph. 5:23, Col. 3:18, 1 Pet. 3:5.

19. Wesley, *Christian Library*, 12:294.

20. Ibid., 329.

21. Wesley, *Journals and Diaries I*, 496.

22. Wesley, *New Testament*, Eph. 5:22, 24, Tit. 2:5.

23. Wesley, *Christian Library*, 12:334.

24. Ibid., 12:299.

25. Ibid., 12:300.

26. Ibid., 12:303–10.

27. Ibid., 12:310.

28. Ibid., 12:310–11, 314–16.

29. Ibid., 12:317.

30. Ibid., 12:317.

31. Ibid., 12:318–19.

32. Ibid., 12:319.

33. Ibid., 12:322–23.

34. Specifically, these references occur in the blessing immediately after the minister pronounces the couple husband and wife, the prayer asking God's blessing on the ongoing spiritual pilgrimage of the husband and wife, and the final blessing at the end of the service. Spirituality in this section, refers to the condition of a person's relationship with God.

35. Wesley, *Christian Library*, 12:270–71, 275–78.

36. Wesley, *Works*, 12:374.

37. Wesley, *Letters*, 5:72.

38. Ibid., 3:91–92.

39. Wesley, *New Testament*, 1 Tim. 3:4.

40. Wesley, *Old Testament*, 1:71.

41. Ibid., 1:74.

42. Ibid., 1:266.

43. Ibid., 1:620, 2:1518.

44. Wesley, *Christian Library*, 12:269–70.

45. Wesley, *New Testament*, Eph. 5:25.

46. Wesley, *Christian Library*, 12:272.

47. Ibid., 12:273.

48. Ibid., 12:275.
49. Stone, *Family, Sex, and Marriage*, 60.
50. Gillis, *For Better, For Worse*, 136.
51. Richard P. Heitzenrater, *The Elusive Mr. Wesley*, vol. 1, *John Wesley His Own Biographer* (Nashville, Tenn.: Abingdon Press, 1984), 185. Notice that the bride's income is reported, but not her name!
52. Gillis, "Married But Not Churched," 38.
53. Stone, *Family, Sex, and Marriage*, 244.
54. Ayling, *John Wesley*, 215.
55. Wesley, *Christian Library*, 12:325–27.
56. Wesley, *Letters*, 5:109.
57. Wesley, *New Testament*, 1 Cor. 7:33.
58. Wesley, *Christian Library*, 12:327–28.
59. Ibid., 12:291–92.
60. Ibid., 12:293–94.
61. Wesley, *Old Testament*, 3:1892.
62. Wesley, *Christian Library*, 12:297.
63. Ibid., 12:298.
64. Ibid., 12:280, 282.
65. Ibid., 12:283–84.
66. Ibid., 12:284–85.
67. Ibid., 12:287.
68. Ibid., 12:289–90.
69. Ibid., 12:291.
70. Ibid., 12:336–38.
71. Ayling, *John Wesley*, 119, 121; C. T. Winchester, *The Life of John Wesley* (New York: MacMillan Co., 1927), 163.
72. Ayling, *John Wesley*, 60, 120–21, 261; Winchester, *The Life of John Wesley*, 163.
73. Ayling, *John Wesley*, 42; Winchester, *The Life of John Wesley*, 163.
74. Ayling, *John Wesley*, 42, 121; Winchester, *The Life of John Wesley*, 164.
75. Ayling, *John Wesley*, 25, 38–40.
76. Ibid., 119–20.
77. Ibid., 55, 138–39; Wesley, *Journal*, 8:146–51; Winchester, *The Life of John Wesley*, 164.
78. Ayling, *John Wesley*, 55–56, 121, 260; Wesley, *Journal*, 8:151–52; Winchester, *The Life of John Wesley*, 164.
79. Ayling, *John Wesley*, 260–61, 314.
80. Samuel J. Rogal, "John Wesley Takes a Wife," *Methodist History* 27 (October 1988): 50.
81. Ayling, *John Wesley*, 216; Rogal, "John Wesley Takes a Wife," 50.
82. Rogal, "John Wesley Takes a Wife," 50.
83. Wesley, *Journal*, 3:512–13.
84. Ibid., 513.
85. It was not unusual for Wesley to omit important information about his private life from his published journals. The accounts of Wesley's romances with Sophy Hopkey and Grace Murray are taken, for the most part, from his private diaries rather than from any autobiographical writings published during Wesley's lifetime. Unfortunately, the private diaries that might contain information about his wedding have been lost.

86. Wesley, *Journal*, 3:513, 515. This information comes from the editor's notes, not from the text of the journal.

87. Meredith, *The Real John Wesley*, 328.

88. Rogal, "John Wesley Takes a Wife," 50.

89. Charles Wesley, *Journal*, 2:78.

90. Wesley, *Journal*, 3:515. Excerpts from Charles Wesley's journal are included in this edition of John Wesley's journal.

91. Ibid.

92. Ibid.

93. Ibid., 3:515–16.

94. Ibid., 3:516–17.

95. Ibid., 3:517.

96. Ibid.

97. Wesley, *Works*, 12:176.

98. Ibid., 12:182–83.

99. Ibid., 12:183–84.

100. Heitzenrater, *The Elusive Mr. Wesley*, 1:191–92.

101. Wesley, *Works*, 12:220–21.

102. Ibid., 12:221.

103. Heitzenrater, *The Elusive Mr. Wesley*, 1:192–93.

104. Ibid., 1:193.

105. Rogal, "John Wesley Takes a Wife," 52.

106. Heitzenrater, *The Elusive Mr. Wesley*, 1:188–90.

107. Wesley, *Letters*, 4:89.

108. Ibid., 4:200, 5:21.

109. Rogal, "John Wesley Takes a Wife," 53.

110. "I did not leave her; I did not send her away; I will not call her back." Wesley, *Works*, 3:423.

111. Heitzenrater, *The Elusive Mr. Wesley*, 1:194.

112. Meredith, *The Real John Wesley*, 338–40.

113. Wesley, *Letters*, 6:321–22.

114. Rogal, "John Wesley Takes a Wife," 53.

115. Wesley, *Works*, 4:218.

116. Rogal, "John Wesley Takes a Wife," 48–49.

117. Kenneth J. Collins, "John Wesley's Relationship with His Wife as Revealed in His Correspondence," *Methodist History* 32 (October 1993): 4; Rogal, 48–49.

118. Collins, "Wesley's Relationship with His Wife," 17–18.

119. Leger, *Wesley's Last Love*, 189.

120. Heitzenrater, *The Elusive Mr. Wesley*, 2:152–53.

121. Wesley, *Letters*, 8:223.

Conclusions

1. Stevenson, *Nuptial Blessing*, 134.

2. Ayling, *John Wesley*, 216–17.

3. *The Journal and Letters of Francis Asbury*, eds. Elmer T. Clark, J. Manning Potts, and Jacob S. Payton, 3 vols. (London: Epworth Press, 1958; Nashville, Tenn.: Abingdon Press, 1958), 2:591.

4. E. Dale Dunlap, "The United Methodist System of Itinerant Ministry," in *Rethinking Methodist History: A Bicentennial Historical Consultation*, ed. Russell R. Richey and Kenneth E. Rowe (Nashville, Tenn.: Kingswood Books, 1985), 23.

5. Ibid.

6. Wesley, *Letters*, 2:91, as quoted in Frederick E. Maser, *The Story of John Wesley's Sisters, or Seven Sisters in Search of Love* (Rutland, Vt.: Academy Books, 1988), 92.

7. Maser, *Wesley's Sisters*, 92.

8. Pamela D. Couture, *Blessed Are the Poor? Women's Poverty, Family Policy, and Practical Theology* (Nashville, Tenn.: Abingdon Press, 1991), 124.

9. Leger, *Wesley's Last Love*, 105.

Appendix A

1. Wesley, *Sunday Service*, 149–55.

2. *The Book of Common Prayer and Administration of the Sacraments, and Other Rites and Ceremonies of the Church, According to the Use of the Church of England* (Oxford: Thomas Baskett, 1753).

Appendix B

1. *The Holy Bible, Containing the Old and New Testaments: Newly Translated out of the Original Tongues, And with the former Translations diligently Compared and Revised* (Oxford: Thomas Basket, 1753).

Selected Bibliography

Bibliographies

Baker, Frank. "Unfolding John Wesley: A Survey of Twenty Years' Studies in Wesley's Thought." *Quarterly Review* 1 (fall 1980): 44–58.

———. *A Union Catalogue of the Publications of John and Charles Wesley.* Durham, N. C., 1966.

Field, Clive D. "Bibliography of Methodist Historical Literature." *Supplement to the Proceedings of The Wesley Historical Society* (May 1989).

Green, Richard. *The Works of John and Charles Wesley: A Bibliography.* 2d ed. London: Methodist Publishing House, 1906.

Hardman, Keith J. "A Checklist of Doctoral Dissertations on Methodist, Evangelical United Brethren, and Related Subjects, 1912–1968." *Methodist History* 8 (April 1970): 38–42.

Jarboe, Betty M. *John and Charles Wesley: A Bibliography.* ATLA Bibliography Series, no. 22. Metuchen, N. J.: American Theological Library Association & Scarecrow Press, 1987.

Lenhart, Thomas E., and Frederick A. Norwood. *A Checklist of Wesleyan and Methodist Studies 1970–1975.* Evanston, Ill.: Institute for Methodist Studies and Related Movements, 1976.

Melton, J. Gordon. "An Annotated Bibliography of Publications about the Life and Work of John Wesley." *Methodist History* 7 (July 1969): 29–46.

Norwood, Frederick A. "Methodist Historical Studies 1930–1959." *Church History* 28 (December 1959): 391–417.

———. "Wesleyan Methodist Historical Studies, 1960–70: A Bibliographical Article." *Methodist History* 10 (January 1972): 23–44.

"Supplement to Checklist of Doctoral Dissertations on Methodist and Related Subjects." *Methodist History* 10 (April 1972): 59–60.

"Supplementary Checklist of Doctoral Dissertations on Methodist and Related Subjects." *Methodist History* 9 (April 1971): 53–61.

Books

Abbey, Charles J., and John H. Overton. *The English Church in the Eighteenth Century.* London: Longmans, Green & Co., 1896.

Abelove, Henry. *The Evangelist of Desire: John Wesley and the Methodists.* Stanford, Calif.: Stanford University Press, 1990.

Asbury, Francis. *The Journals and Letters of Francis Asbury.* Ed. Elmer T. Clark, J. Manning Potts, and Jacob S. Payton. 3 vols. London: Epworth Press; Nashville, Tenn.: Abingdon Press, 1958.

Ayling, Stanley, *John Wesley*. Nashville, Tenn.: Abingdon Press, 1979.

Baker, Frank. *Charles Wesley: As Revealed by His Letters*. London: Epworth Press, 1948.

————. *John Wesley and the Church of England*. Nashville, Tenn.: Abingdon Press, 1970.

Barstow, Anne Llewellyn. "An Ambiguous Legacy: Anglican Clergy Wives after the Reformation," in *Women in New Worlds: Historical Perspectives on the Wesleyan Tradition*. Vol. 2. Edited by Rosemary Skinner Keller, Louise L. Queen, and Hilah F. Thomas. Nashville: Abingdon, 1982.

Belmont, Nicole. "The Symbolic Function of the Wedding Procession in the Popular Rituals of Marriage." In *Rituals, Religion, and the Sacred: Selections from the Annales Economies, Societes, Civilisations*, ed. Robert Forster and Orest Ranum, trans. Elborg Forster and Patricia M. Ranum. Vol. 7. Baltimore: Johns Hopkins University Press, 1982.

Biddle, Perry H., Jr. *Abingdon Marriage Manual*. Nashville, Tenn.: Abingdon, 1974.

Black, Henry Campbell. *Black's Law Dictionary: Definitions of the Terms and Phrases of American and English Jurisprudence, Ancient and Modern*. Revised Fourth Edition. St. Paul, Minn.: West Publishing Co., 1968.

Blaisdell, Charmarie Jenkins. "The Matrix of Reform: Women in the Lutheran and Calvinist Movements." In *Triumph Over Silence: Women in Protestant History*, ed. Richard L. Greaves. Westport, Conn.: Greenwood Press, 1985.

Borgen, Ole E. *John Wesley on the Sacraments*. Grand Rapids, Mich.: Francis Asbury Press, 1972.

Bowmer, John C. *The Sacrament of the Lord's Supper in Early Methodism*. Westminster, England; Dacre Press, 1951.

Brailsford, Mabel Richmond. *A Tale of Two Brothers: John and Charles Wesley*. New York: Oxford University Press, 1954.

Brauer, Jerald C. *The Westminster Dictionary of Church History*. Philadelphia: Westminster Press, 1971.

Brightman, F. E. *The English Rite: Being a Synopsis of the Sources and Revisions of The Book of Common Prayer with an Introduction and an Appendix*. 2 vols. London: Rivingtons, 1915.

Brown, Earl Kent. *Women of Mr. Wesley's Methodism*. Studies in Women and Religion, vol. 11. New York: Edwin Mellen Press, 1983.

Certain Sermons: Appointed by the Queen's Majesty to Be Declared and Read by All Parsons, Vicars, and Curates, Every Sunday and Holiday in Their Churches; and by Her Grace's Advice Perused and Overseen for the Better Understanding of the Simple People. Cambridge: John W. Parker, 1850.

Clarke, W. K. Lowther, and Charles Harris, eds. *Liturgy and Worship: A Companion to the Prayer Books of the Anglican Communion*. New York: Macmillan Co., 1932.

Companion to "The Book of Services": Introduction, Commentary, and Instructions for Using the New United Methodist Services. Nashville, Tenn.: Abingdon Press, 1988.

Cooke, Richard Joseph. *History of the Ritual of the Methodist Episcopal Church*. Cincinnati, Ohio: Jennings & Pye, 1900.

Cooper, Joseph. *The Love Stories of John Wesley*. Boston: Gorham Press, 1931.

Couture, Pamela D. *Blessed Are the Poor? Women's Poverty, Family Policy, and Practical Theology.* Nashville, Tenn.: Abingdon Press, 1991.

Cuming, G. J. *A History of Anglican Liturgy.* London: Macmillan, 1969.

Daniel, Evan. *The Prayer-Book: Its History, Language, and Contents.* 22d ed. London: Wells Gardner, Darton & Co., 1909.

Davies, Horton. *Worship and Theology in England: From Watts and Wesley to Maurice, 1690–1850.* Princeton: Princeton University Press, 1961.

————. *The Worship of the English Puritans.* Westminster, England: Dacre Press, 1948.

Davies, J. G., ed. *The New Westminster Dictionary of Liturgy and Worship.* Philadelphia: Westminster Press, 1986. S.v. "Marriage: Medieval and Roman Catholic," by J. D. Crichton, and "Marriage: Methodist," by James F. White.

Dearmer, Percy. *The Story of the Prayer Book: In the Old and New World and Throughout the Anglican Church.* London: Oxford University Press, 1933.

Drakeford, John W. *Take Her, Mr. Wesley.* Waco, Tex.: Word Books, 1973.

Dunlap, E. Dale. "The United Methodist System of Itinerant Ministry." In *Rethinking Methodist History: A Bicentennial Historical Consultation,* ed. Russell E. Richey and Kenneth E. Rowe. Nashville, Tenn.: Kingswood Books, 1985.

Edwards, Maldwyn. *My Dear Sister: The Story of John Wesley and the Women in His Life.* Manchester, England: Penwork, n.d.

The First Prayer-Book of Edward VI. Compared with the Successive Revisions of "The Book of Common Prayer": also a Concordance to the Rubricks in the Several Editions. Oxford: James Parker & Co., 1877.

The First Prayer-Book of King Edward VI. London: Griffith, Farran, Okeden & Welsh, n.d.

Flint, Charles Wesley. *Charles Wesley and His Colleagues.* With introductory notes by Gerald Kennedy, G. Bromley Oxnam and Norman Vincent Peale. Washington, D. C.: Public Affairs Press, 1957.

Garber, Paul Neff. *The Methodist Meeting House.* New York: Board of Missions and Church Extension, The Methodist Church, 1941.

Gill, Frederick C. *Charles Wesley: The First Methodist.* New York: Abingdon Press, 1964.

————. *In the Steps of John Wesley.* New York: Abingdon Press, 1962.

Gillis, John R. *For Better, For Worse: British Marriages, 1600 to the Present.* New York: Oxford University Press, 1985.

Goodsell, Willystine. *A History of Marriage and the Family.* Rev. ed. New York: Macmillan Co., 1934.

Greven, Philip. *The Protestant Temperament: Patterns of Child-Rearing, Religious Experience, and the Self in Early America.* New York: Alfred A. Knopf, 1977.

Green, V. H. H. *John Wesley.* London: Thomas Nelson & Sons, 1964.

Haddal, Ingvar. *John Wesley: A Biography.* New York: Abingdon Press, 1961.

Harmon, Nolan B., Jr. *The Rites and Ritual of Episcopal Methodism: With Particular Reference to the Rituals of the Methodist Episcopal Church and the Methodist Episcopal Church, South, Respectively.* Nashville, Tenn.: Publishing House of the M. E. Church, South, 1926.

————, ed. *The Encyclopedia of World Methodism.* Vol. 2. Nashville, Tenn.: United Methodist Publishing House, 1974. S.v. "Marriage," by Nolan B. Harmon, Jr.

Harrison, G. Elsie. *Son to Susanna: The Private Life of John Wesley*. Nashville, Tenn.: Cokesbury Press, 1938.

Hayes, Alan L. "John Wesley and Sophy Hopkey: A Case Study in Wesley's Attitude Toward Women. In *Women in New Worlds: Historical Perspectives on the Wesleyan Tradition*, Ed. Rosemary Skinner Keller, Louise L. Queen, and Hilah F. Thomas. 2 vols. Nashville, Tenn.: Abingdon, 1982.

Heitzenrater, Richard P. *The Elusive Mr. Wesley*. 2 vols. Nashville, Tenn.: Abingdon Press, 1984.

Hickman, Hoyt L., ed. *Worship Resources of The United Methodist Hymnal*. Nashville, Tenn.: Abingdon Press, 1989.

The Holy Bible, Containing the Old and New Testaments: Newly Translated out of the Original Tongues, and with the Former Translations Diligently Compared and Revised. Oxford: Thomas Baskett, 1753.

Hooker, Richard. *Of the Laws of Ecclesiastical Polity*. London: J. M. Dent & Sons, 1922.

Hoon, Paul W. "The Order for the Service of Marriage." In *Companion to "The Book of Worship"*, ed. William F. Dunkle, Jr. and Joseph D. Quillian, Jr. Nashville, Tenn.: Abingdon Press, 1970.

Jackson, Thomas. *The Life of the Rev. Charles Wesley, M. A. Some Time Student of Christ-Church, Oxford: Comprising A Review of His Poetry; Sketches of the Rise and Progress of Methodism, with Notices of Contemporary Events and Characters*. New York; G. Lane & P. P. Sandford, 1844.

Johnson, James Turner. *A Society Ordained by God: English Puritan Marriage Doctrine in the First Half of the Seventeenth Century*. Studies in Christian Ethics Series. Nashville, Tenn.: Abingdon Press, 1970.

Jones, D. M. *Charles Wesley: A Study*. London: Skefington & Sons, n.d.

Joyce, George Hayward. *Christian Marriage: An Historical and Doctrinal Study*. 2d ed., rev. and enl. London: Sheed & Ward, 1948.

Keller, Rosemary Skinner, Louise L. Queen, and Hilah F. Thomas, eds. *Women in New Worlds: Historical Perspectives on the Wesleyan Tradition*. 2 vols. Nashville, Tenn.: Abingdon, 1982.

Lacey, T. A. *Marriage in Church and State*. Fully revised and supplemented by R. C. Mortimer. London: S. P. C. K., 1959.

Larrabee, Wm. C. *Wesley and His Coadjutors*, ed. B. F. Tefft. 2 vols. Cincinnati, Ohio: Swormstedt & Power, 1851.

Laver, James. *Wesley*. New York: D. Appleton & Co., 1933.

Lawson, A. B. *John Wesley and the Christian Ministry: The Sources and Development of His Opinions and Practices*. London: S. P. C. K., 1963.

Lee, Bernard J., ed. *Alternative Futures for Worship*. Vol. 5, *Christian Marriage*, ed. Bernard Cooke. Collegeville, Minn.: Liturgical Press, 1987.

Lee, Umphrey. *John Wesley and Modern Religion*. Nashville, Tenn.: Cokesbury Press, 1936.

————. *The Lord's Horseman*. New York: Century Co., 1928.

Leger, J. A. *John Wesley's Last Love*. London: J. M. Dent & Sons, 1910.

Legg, J. Wickham, ed. *The Sarum Missal: Edited from Three Early Manuscripts*. Oxford: Clarendon Press, 1916. Reprint, Oxford: University Press, 1969.

Lipsky, Abram. *John Wesley: A Portrait*. New York: Simon & Schuster, 1928.

Lunn, Arnold. *John Wesley.* With a Foreword by S. Parkes Cadman. New York: Dial Press, 1929.

Maser, Frederick E. *The Story of John Wesley's Sisters, or Seven Sisters in Search of Love.* Rutland, Vt.: Academy Books, 1988.

McConnell, Francis J. *John Wesley.* New York: Abingdon Press, 1939.

McDonald, William. *The Young People's Wesley.* With an introduction by W. F. Mallalieu. Cincinnati, Ohio: Jennings & Pye, 1901.

McGinn, Donald Joseph. *The Admonition Controversy.* New Brunswick, N. J.: Rutgers University Press, 1949.

Menefee, Samuel Pyeatt. *Wives for Sale: An Ethnographic Study of British Popular Divorce.* New York: St. Martin's Press, 1981.

Meredith, William Henry. *The Real John Wesley.* Cincinnati, Ohio: Jennings & Pye, 1903.

Miller, L. David. *Hymns: The Story of Christian Song.* Philadelphia: Lutheran Church Press, 1969.

Monk, Robert C. *John Wesley: His Puritan Heritage.* Nashville, Tenn.: Abingdon Press, 1966.

Moore, Robert L. *John Wesley and Authority: A Psychological Perspective.* American Academy of Religion Dissertation Series, no. 29. Ann Arbor, Mich.: Edwards Bros., 1979.

Murstein, Bernard I. *Love, Sex, and Marriage Through the Ages.* With a foreword by William M. Kephart. New York: Springer Publishing Co., 1974.

Nave, Orville J. *Nave's Topical Bible: A Digest of the Holy Scriptures.* Nashville, Tenn.: Southwestern Co., 1962.

Newton, John A. "Wesley and Women." In *John Wesley: Contemporary Perspectives,* ed. John Stacey. With an introduction by Frank Baker. London: Epworth Press, 1988.

Norwood, Frederick A. *The Story of American Methodism: A History of the United Methodists and Their Relations.* Nashville, Tenn.: Abingdon Press, 1974.

————, ed. *The Methodist Discipline of 1798: Including the Annotations of Thomas Coke and Francis Asbury.* Rutland, Vt.: Academy Books, 1979.

Nuelsen, John L. *John Wesley and the German Hymn.* Translated by Theo Parry, Sydney H. Moore, and Arthur Holbrook. Calverly, England: A. S. Holbrook, 1972.

Overton, J. H. *John Wesley.* English Leaders of Religion, ed. A. M. M. Stedman. London: Methuen & Co., 1891.

Overton, John H., and Frederic Relton. *The English Church: From the Accession of George I. to the End of the Eighteenth Century (1714–1800).* London: Macmillan & Co., 1906.

Ozment, Steven. *The Age of Reform 1250–1550: An Intellectual and Religious History of Late Medieval and Reformation Europe.* New Haven: Yale University Press, 1980.

Procter, Francis. *A New History of "The Book of Common Prayer."* Revised and rewritten by Walter Howard Frere. London: Macmillan & Co., 1955.

Pullan, Leighton. *The History of "The Book of Common Prayer."* London: Longmans, Green, & Co., 1914.

Rack, Henry D. *Reasonable Enthusiast: John Wesley and the Rise of Methodism.* 2d ed. Nashville, Tenn.: Abingdon Press, 1992.

Rattenbury, J. Ernest. *The Eucharistic Hymns of John and Charles Wesley*. London: Epworth Press, 1948.

————. *Wesley's Legacy to the World: Six Studies in the Permanent Values of the Evangelical Revival*. London: Epworth Press, 1928.

Rigg, James H. *The Living Wesley: As He Was in His Youth and in His Prime*. With an introduction by John F. Hurst. New York: Nelson & Phillips, 1874.

Rowe, Kenneth E., ed. *The Place of Wesley in the Christian Tradition*. Metuchen, N. J.: Scarecrow Press, 1976.

Rogal, Samuel J. *John and Charles Wesley*. Boston: Twayne Publishers, 1983.

Sauer, Charles A. *A Pocket Story of John Wesley*. Nashville, Tenn.: Tidings, 1967; reprint, Nashville, Tenn.: Discipleship Resources, 1976.

Schillebeeckx, Edward. *Marriage: Human Reality and Saving Mystery*. Trans. N. D. Smith, 2 vols. New York: Sheed & Ward, 1965.

Schmidt, Martin. *John Wesley: A Theological Biography*. Trans. Norman P. Goldhawk. 2 vols. New York: Abingdon Press, 1962.

Scott, Donald M., and Bernard Wishy, eds. *America's Families: A Documentary History*. New York: Harper & Row, 1982.

Searle, Mark, and Kenneth W. Stevenson. *Documents of the Marriage Liturgy*. Collegeville, Minn.: The Liturgical Press, 1992.

A Service of Christian Marriage: With Introduction, Commentary, and Additional Resources. Nashville, Tenn.: United Methodist Publishing House, 1979.

Shepherd, Massey Hamilton, Jr. *The Oxford American Prayer Book Commentary*. New York: Oxford University Press, 1950.

Simon, John S. *John Wesley: The Last Phase*. London: Epworth Press, 1934.

Snow, M. Lawrence. *Planning a Christian Wedding*. Nashville, Tenn.: Discipleship Resources, 1988.

Southey, Robert. *The Life of Wesley; And Rise and Progress of Methodism*. Ed. Charles Cuthbert Southey. 2d American ed. 2 vols. New York: Harper & Bros., 1847.

Sovik, E. A. *Architecture for Worship*. Minneapolis, Minn.: Augsburg Publishing House, 1973.

Squire, Russel N. *Church Music: Musical and Hymnological Developments in Western Christianity*. St. Louis, Mo.: Bethany Press, 1962.

Stevens, Abel. *The Women of Methodism: Its Three Foundresses, Susanna Wesley, The Countess of Huntingdon, and Barbara Heck; with Sketches of Their Female Associates and Successors in the Early History of Denominations*. New York: Carlton & Lanahan, 1869.

Stevenson, George J. *Memorials of the Wesley Family*. New York: Nelson & Phillips, 1876.

Stevenson, Kenneth. *Nuptial Blessing: A Study of Christian Marriage Rites*. New York: Oxford University Press, 1983.

Stone, Lawrence. *The Family, Sex and Marriage in England 1500–1800*. New York: Harper & Row, 1977.

Swinburne, Henry. *A Treatise of Spousals or Matrimonial Contracts: Wherein All the Questions Relating to the Subject are ingeniously Debated and Resolved*. London: S. Roycroft for Robert Clavell, 1686.

Szews, George R. *We Will Celebrate a Church Wedding*. Collegeville, Minn.: Liturgical Press, 1983.

Talafous, Don. *Planning a Christian Wedding.* Collegeville, Minn.: Liturgical Press, 1985.

Telford, John. *The Life of John Wesley.* New York: Eaton & Mains, n.d.

Thompson, Bard. *Liturgies of the Western Church.* Philadelphia: Fortress Press, 1961.

Treatise of Femme Coverts: or, The Lady's Law Containing All the Laws and Statutes relating to Women. London: E. & R. Nutt & R. Gosling, for B. Lintot, 1732.

Tuttle, Robert G. *John Wesley: His Life and Theology.* Grand Rapids, Mich.: Zondervan Publishing House, 1978.

Tyerman, L. *The Life and Times of the Rev. John Wesley, M. A., Founder of the Methodists.* 3 vols. New York: Harper & Bros., 1872.

The United Methodist Book of Worship. Nashville, Tenn.: United Methodist Publishing House, 1992.

The United Methodist Hymnal: Book of United Methodist Worship. Nashville, Tenn.: United Methodist Publishing House, 1989.

Vulliamy, C. E. *John Wesley.* New York: Charles Scribner's Sons, 1932.

Wade, John Donald. *John Wesley.* New York: Coward-McCann, 1930.

Wakely, J. B. *Anecdotes of the Wesleys.* New York: Carlton & Lanahan, 1869.

Watson, Richard. *The Life of the Rev. John Wesley, A.M.* 1st American official ed. New York: B. Waugh & T. Mason, 1836.

Wedgwood, Julia. *John Wesley and the Evangelical Reaction of the Eighteenth Century.* London: Macmillan & Co., 1870.

Whitaker, E. C. *Martin Bucer and The Book of Common Prayer.* Great Wakering, England: Mayhew-McCrimmon, 1974.

White, James F. *A Brief History of Christian Worship.* Nashville, Tenn.: Abingdon Press, 1993.

————. *Documents of Christian Worship: Descriptive and Interpretive Sources.* Louisville, Ky.: Westminster/John Knox Press, 1992.

————. *Introduction to Christian Worship.* Rev. ed. Nashville, Tenn.: Abingdon Press, 1990.

————. *Protestant Worship and Church Architecture: Theological and Historical Considerations.* New York: Oxford University Press, 1964.

Whitehead, John. *The Life of the Rev. John Wesley, M.A.* With an introduction by Thomas H. Stockton. 2d American ed. 2 vols. Philadelphia: William S. Stockton, 1845.

Wilder, Franklin. *The Methodist Riots: The Testing of Charles Wesley.* Great Neck, N. Y.: Todd & Honeywell, 1981.

Willimon, William H., and Robert L. Wilson. *Preaching and Worship in the Small Church.* Creative Leadership Series, ed. Lyle E. Schaller. Nashville, Tenn.: Abingdon, 1980.

Winchester, C. T. *The Life of John Wesley.* New York: Macmillan Co., 1927.

Periodicals

Baker, Frank. "John Wesley's First Marriage." *The Duke Divinity School Review* 31 (autumn 1966): 175–88.

————. "Some Observations on John Wesley's Relationship with Grace Murray." *Methodist History* 16 (October 1977): 42–45.

Barstow, Anne Llewellyn. "The First Generations of Anglican Clergy Wives: Heroines or Whores?" *Historical Magazine of the Protestant Episcopal Church* 52 (March 1983): 3–16.

Collins, Kenneth J. "John Wesley's Relationship with His Wife as Revealed by His Correspondence." *Methodist History* 32 (October 1993): 4–18.

Davies, Gaius. "The Puritan Teaching on Marriage and the Family." *The Evangelical Quarterly* 27 (1955): 15–30.

Despland, Michel. "Norms and Models in Early Modern France and England: A Study in Comparative Ethics." *The Journal of Religious Ethics* 10 (spring 1982): 68–102.

Donelson, Paul G. "The Rites of the Church: To Whom Do You Say 'No'?" *Circuit Rider* 11 (July–August 1987): 10–11.

Edwards, Maldwyn. "The Reluctant Lover: John Wesley as Suitor." *Methodist History* 12 (January 1974): 46–62.

Elmen, Paul. "On Worshiping the Bride." *Anglican Theological Review* 68 (July 1986): 241–49.

George, A. Raymond. "The Sunday Service." *Proceedings of The Wesley Historical Society* 40 (February 1976): 102–5.

Gillis, John R. "Married But Not Churched: Plebeian Sexual Relations and Marital Nonconformity in Eighteenth-Century Britain." *Eighteenth Century Life*, n.s., 9, no. 3 (May 1985): 31–42.

Gregorio, Robert. "A History of Christian Marriage." *Liturgy* 4, no. 2 (spring 1984): 37–43.

Haller, William, and Malleville Haller. "The Puritan Art of Love." *The Huntington Library Quarterly* 5 (January 1942): 235–72.

Harmon, Nolan B., Jr., "John Wesley's 'Sunday Service' and Its American Revisions." *Proceedings of the Wesley Historical Society* 39 (June 1974): 137–44.

Harmon, Paul Wesley. "Wilt Thou Have This Woman to Be Thy Mother?" *Circuit Rider* 7 (March 1983): 15–16.

Hunter, Frederick. "Sources of Wesley's Revision of the Prayer Book in 1784–8." *Proceedings of The Wesley Historical Society* 23 (1941–42): 123–33.

Johnson, James T. "English Puritan Thought on the Ends of Marriage." *Church History* 38 (December 1969): 429–36.

Katschke-Jennings, Bertha. "Some Church Historical Perspectives on Divorce and Remarriage." *American Baptist Quarterly* 3 (March 1984): 42–52.

Maser, Frederick E. "John Wesley's Only Marriage: An Examination of Dr. Frank Baker's Article 'John Wesley's First Marriage.'" *Methodist History* 16 (October 1977): 33–41.

McClanahan, Arthur Lee. "A Covenant Service to Celebrate Love." *Circuit Rider* 8 (March 1984): 11.

Muirhead, I. A. "'The Forme of Marriage': 1562 and Today." *Scottish Journal of Theology* 6 (1953): 31–42.

Nester, Tony R. "Are Pastors Abusing the Marriage Service?" *The Circuit Rider* 2 (March 1978): 20.

Pawson, John. "Extracts from Letters of the Revd. John Pawson, 1762–1806." *Proceedings of The Wesley Historical Society* 11 (1918): 49–54.

Perdue, Harold C. "Should Clergy Perform Weddings for Nonmembers?" *Circuit Rider* 8 (May 1984): 11–12.

Pierce-Higgins, John D. "1549 and All That." *The Modern Churchman*, n.s., 6 (April 1963): 253–54.

Rattenbury, J. Ernest. "Note on Article on 'Sources of Wesley's Revision of the Prayer Book in 1784–8.'" *Proceedings of The Wesley Historical Society* 23 (1941–42): 173–75.

Rogal, Samuel J. "John Wesley Takes a Wife." *Methodist History* 27 (October 1988): 48–55.

Smith, Peter M. "I Publish the Banns of Marriage . . . ." *The Modern Churchman*, n.s., 12 (July 1969): 299–308.

Stevenson, Kenneth. "Marriage Liturgy: Lessons from History." *Anglican Theological Review* 68 (July 1986): 225–40.

Swift, Wesley F. "Methodism and The Book of Common Prayer." *Proceedings of The Wesley Historical Society* 27 (1949–50): 33–41.

————. "The Sunday Service of the Methodists." *Proceedings of The Wesley Historical Society* 29 (March 1953): 12–20.

Tucker, Karen Westerfield. "Liturgical Expressions of Care for the Poor in the Wesleyan Tradition: A Case Study for the Ecumenical Church." *Worship* 69 (1995): 55.

Weems, Lovett Hayes, Jr. "Let's Remove Sexism from Weddings." *Circuit Rider* 5 (April 1981): 3.

White, James F. "Early Methodist Liturgical Architecture." *Motive* 18 (March 1958): 12–13, 19–20.

————. "Toward a Discipline of the Sacraments." *The Circuit Rider* 4 (January 180): 3–7.

Wright, David F. "Woman Before and After the Fall: A Comparison of Luther's and Calvin's Interpretation of Genesis 1–3." *Churchman* 98 (1984): 126–35.

Unpublished Materials

Brown, Earl Kent. "The Women of Methodism." Four addresses delivered at the Lakeside School of Mission, United Methodist Women, East Ohio Conference of the United Methodist Church, Lakeside, Ohio, 16–19 July 1973. Theology Library, Boston University, Boston.

Selleck, Jerald Brian. "'The Book of Common Prayer' in the Theology of John Wesley." Ph.D. diss., Drew University, 1983.

Wade, William Nash. "A History of Public Worship in the Methodist Episcopal Church and Methodist Episcopal Church, South, from 1784 to 1905." Ph.D. diss., University of Notre Dame, 1981.

Works of John and Charles Wesley

Wesley, Charles. *The Journal of the Rev. Charles Wesley, M.A.: Sometime Student of Christ Church, Oxford, to Which Are Appended Selections from His Correspondence and Poetry.* With an introduction and occasional notes by Thomas Jackson. 2 vols. London: John Mason, 1849.

————. *Sayings and Portraits of Charles Wesley: With Family Portraits, Historic*

Scenes, and Additional Portraits of John Wesley. Comp. and ed. by John Telford. London: Epworth Press, 1927.

Wesley, John. *A Christian Library: Consisting of Extracts from and Abridgements of the Choicest Pieces of Practical Divinity Which Have Been Published in the English Tongue.* 30 vols. London: T. Cordeux, 1821.

————. *Explanatory Notes Upon the New Testament.* 2 vols. London: The Wesleyan-Methodist Book Room, n.d.,: Reprint, Grand Rapids: Baker Book House, 1986.

————. *Explanatory Notes Upon the Old Testament.* 3 vols. Bristol: William Pine, 1765: Reprint, Salem, Ohio: Schmul Publishers, 1975.

————. *John Wesley's Prayer Book: The Sunday Service of the Methodists in North America.* With introduction, notes and commentary by James F. White. Cleveland: OSL Publications, 1991.

————. *John Wesley's Sunday Service of the Methodists in North America.* With an introduction by James F. White. The United Methodist Publishing House and the United Methodist Board of Higher Education and Ministry, 1984. n.p.

————. *The Journal of the Rev. John Wesley, A.M.: Enlarged from Original Mss., with Notes from Unpublished Diaries, Annotations, Maps, and Illustrations.* Edited by Nehemiah Curnock. Standard Edition. 8 vols. London: Epworth Press, 1938.

————. *The Letters of the Rev. John Wesley, A.M.* Edited by John Telford. Standard Edition. 8 vols. London: Epworth Press, 1931.

————. *The Sunday Service of the Methodists in North America. With other Occasional Services.* London: 1784: Reprint, Nashville: The United Methodist Publishing House, 1992.

————. *Thoughts on Marriage and a Single Life.* Bristol: Felix Farley, 1743.

————. *Thoughts on the Sin of Onan.* London, 1767.

————. "Unpublished Letters of John Wesley." *Methodist History* 1 (October 1962): 34–38.

————. "An Unpublished Wesley Letter." *Proceedings of The Wesley Historical Society* 39 (June 1974): 144.

————. *Wesley's Standard Sermons.* Ed. Edward H. Sugden. 3rd ed., annotated. 2 vols. London: Epworth Press, 1951.

————. *The Works of John Wesley.* 3d ed., 14 vols. ed. Thomas Jackson. London: Wesleyan Methodist Book Room, 1872: Reprint, Grand Rapids, Mich.: Baker Book House, 1984.

————. *Journals and Diaries I (1735–38).* Vol. 18 of *The Works of John Wesley,* edited by W. Reginald Ward and Richard P. Heitzenrater. Nashville: Abingdon Press, 1988.

Index

Abbey, Charles, 50

Admonition of Matthew Parker, 24–25

Admonition to Parliament, 94

Adultery, 56, 115, 119, 122–23

"Advice to the People Called Methodists with Regard to Dress," 96

Anglican Church: and dancing, 64; and Eucharist, 39–41, 97; and Henry VIII, 152n. 15; and sex, 152n. 12; and wedding rings, 94–96, 98; defended by Hooker, 38; marriage doctrine of, 10–11, 24, 52–55, 57, 126–28; music, 47–51; required for legal marriage, 26–27; role of priest in, 26; standard homilies of, 47; wedding service of, 10, 57. *See also* Book of Common Prayer

Annulment. *See* Divorce and remarriage

Architecture: Church, 44–45, 97

Arranged marriages, 11, 83

Asbury, Francis, 128

Asceticism, 64

Atkins, Will, 114

Attendance at weddings, 10, 16, 44–45

Authority of the husband. *See* Husband, duties of

Baker, Frank, 34

Banns, 10, 18–23, 26, 38, 77

Bennet, John, 30–34, 51, 62, 86, 130

Berridge, John, 71–72

Birth control. *See* Contraception

Bisson, Jane, 89

Blackwell, Ebenezer, 117–20

Bolton, Ann, 89

Book of Common Order, 95

Book of Common Prayer: and impediments to marriage, 22, 26; banns in, 18–19, 22; day and time of marriage in, 38–39; duties of the husband in, 103; eucharist in, 39–44, 97; espousals in, 17–18; giving away of the bride in, 80; included Parker's table, 25; indissolubility of marriage in, 57; location of wedding in, 44–46; obedience of the wife in, 101; purposes of marriage in, 52, 57, 68, 127; revised by Wesley, 9–11, 126; used for engagement, 28; wedding homily in, 46; wedding ring in, 93–96; wedding service changed little, 126

Boyce, John, 27–29

Bride-Bush, A: See Directions for Married Persons

Bride: Giving away of the. *See* Giving away of the bride

Broadwood, Hannah, 32

Broadwood, James, 32

Bucer, Martin, 40, 54, 84, 94–95

Bush, Elijah, 81

Calvin, John, 40, 56

Case of Marriage between Near Relations Considered, 25

Catholic Church. *See* Roman Catholic Church

Causes for marriage, 10–11, 52–79, 127

Causton, Thomas, 72–74, 77–78

Causton, Mrs. Thomas, 72, 77

Celibacy. *See* Continency

Censura, 94

"Character of a Methodist, The," 65

Charles II, 40

Chastity. *See* Continency

Children: as the purpose of marriage, 53–54, 127–28; economic provision for, 109–10; love of parents for, 108–9; of Patty and Westley Hall, 115, 129–30; of unbelievers, 88; parental behavior in the presence of, 105, 111; parental consent to marriage of, 80–83; raising of, 53–54, 107, 110–11;

172